STRIDES BETWEEN US

Marc Cianfarani

For my wife and children, whose love and support guided every step. For Dolce, my whippet who inspired many touching moments in this story.

And for all the Jakes in this world, those who have had to struggle, fight and rise again.

Author's Note

This is a work of fiction.

Jake's story came to me gradually. It wasn't from a single source or conversation, but from years of paying attention to the people cities tend to overlook. The person whose identity was built around a body that one day stopped cooperating.

All characters and institutions in this novel are invented. Springfield University exists only on these pages. Names, characters, businesses, organizations, places, events, and incidents are either the product of the author's imagination or uses fictitiously. Any resemblance to actual persons, living or dead, or actual events is purely coincidental.

If this story feels true, that is the aim of fiction, to illuminate.

Chapter One

Jake lay half-wrapped in a frayed blanket with his back pressed to the cold stone of a retaining wall. One foot extended awkwardly from an old running shoe whose sole had nearly peeled off. The shoe didn't match the other one.

A passing bus rumbled somewhere in the distance. A pigeon fluttered down nearby, pecking at crumbs. Jake blinked awake. His joints protested as he sat up, and he stretched his injured leg until the pain settled.

Across the path, bundled in coat layers too big for her, an elderly homeless woman sat hunched over a cold cup of coffee. She smiled a tired smile when Jake lifted a hand in greeting.

Jake stood, dusting leaves from his clothes. He limped towards the nearby garbage bin, even if he wasn't hungry yet.

Inside the bin, on top of a cardboard box, he found a slice of discarded pizza, still wrapped, still good.

Jake didn't hesitate to walk it over to the elderly woman. Lowering himself to her level, he placed the slice gently in her hands.

"You should eat," he said softly.

She touched his wrist and looked at him like someone who had stopped expecting anything from anyone. Jake didn't stay to watch her finish. He never did.

Jake continued down the path, the limp more pronounced in the cold morning air. The park filled with early risers. He saw a few joggers and a dog walker with four labradoodles and a French bulldog moving through the trail. And then he saw them: two college-aged runners bursting down the trail, strides strong, running that felt effortless.

Jake stopped walking. The rhythmic slap-slap-slap of the runners' shoes faded down the path, but the sound didn't die. It grew louder until it wasn't the dull thud of pavement anymore. It was the biting crunch of spikes digging into a synthetic track.

The smell of damp autumn leaves vanished, replaced by the scent of a college track.

He was rounding the final curve, legs driving, the world narrowing to the finish line and the sound of the crowd. The coach was screaming to shorten his stride, but Jake tuned him out. He only had eyes for the bleachers.

Paige was there, in her yellow top, the good luck one she always wore to his meets. And in her arms Emily. Tiny, perfect Emily, her small hands clapping, her mouth open in a cheer he couldn't hear.

He surged forward, the finish line waiting. He planted his right foot, ready to launch into the final sprint. Then, a sound like a dry branch snapping inside a tunnel. There was no pain at first, a sickening lack of resistance. He hit the track hard, the grit scraping his cheek. Then the pain arrived, deep and severe unlike anything he had ever experienced. The cheering stopped. The silence was worse.

Through the haze, he saw Paige stand up, the joy on her face curdling into a mask of pure terror. She screamed his name, but it sounded like she was underwater.

The stadium lights flickered and died, leaving only the grey haze of the park. The roar of the crowd thinned out, replaced by the hiss of a bus's air brakes three blocks over.

He was standing on the asphalt path, his chest heaving.

He rubbed his knee instinctively, his fingers tracing the scar through the fabric of his pants. He kept walking, trying to lose himself in the everyday rhythms of the park.

He reached his usual bench, his temporary "home," if one could call it that. A grocery cart stood beside it, filled with blankets, a jacket he'd found early last winter, a water bottle, and a few other belongings that survived the streets with him.

He sat, letting the morning settle into him. He tried to breathe slow.

He didn't sit long. He turned towards the row of bakeries three blocks over. If he was fast, he'd reach the bins before the day-old sourdough was buried under the weight of the morning's trash.

The alley behind the Midtown Fitness Center always smelled faintly of rubber mats and bleach, a scent Jake used to know well. He pushed his cart, wheels rattling over uneven concrete. Morning light hadn't reached the alley yet; it was still wrapped in a blue-grey chill.

A black garbage bag lay torn open beside the dumpster, shoes and clothing spilling onto the asphalt. Jake normally kept his head down, taking only what he needed, but he paused. Maybe it was the faint familiar outline in the mess. Maybe it was nothing.

He crouched, carefully, because of the leg, and brushed aside a strip of plastic.

A pair of running shoes.

They were used and worn, but were intact, breathable mesh, good soles, laces still strong. He inhaled sharply.

He didn't touch them right away.

The alley noise softened, as he reached out, fingers trembling slightly, and lifted them by the heels. The soles bore the faint imprint of mileage, curves shaped by countless strides. They felt like a relic. Or a ghost.

Jake exhaled long and steady, placing them back on the dumpster lid.

He took a few steps.

He closed his eyes, letting the faint memory stretch through his body. Then he turned back.

He lifted the shoes again, tucked them into the canvas bag strapped to his cart. The bag where he kept the few things that still mattered. He didn't put them on. Not that morning, or that day.

But as he pushed the cart out of the alley, the city hummed around him, and in the corner of his mind he saw it: a soccer ball skidding across grass, sharp cuts, long strides and at the edge of his vision, a young whippet dashing past, ears back, paws barely touching the ground.

Jake blinked, and suddenly he was there.

Fourteen years earlier

Chapter Two

A handful of teenagers moved across the grass in loose formation, laughter cutting through the morning air as the ball skipped and rolled between them. The soccer field ran alongside a narrow walking trail where a few people were walking their dogs.

Jake sprinted down the sideline, chased the ball into the corner, and cut back sharply. On a few plays, his speed separated him completely. Long, effortless strides that seemed to pull the air behind him. He didn't notice who was watching.

Coach Roberts walked the trail with a young whippet trotting eagerly at his side. He wasn't paying much attention until a flash at the edge of his vision. He slowed, then stopped altogether, eyes tracking the boy on the field. Jake accelerated cleanly, naturally.

Roberts stayed where he was. He watched the game play out from a distance, hands resting loosely on the leash, curiosity keeping him still.

After a few minutes, the game slowed as the players gathered briefly near the sideline. Coach Roberts crouched and unclipped Dolce's leash. "Go on, show us what you've got," he said.

In an instant, Dolce cut hard between cones, paws

barely kissing the grass before she was gone in a new direction. Jake's eyes followed her every move at the corner of his vision, and his chest tightened with the same pulse he felt while running. The rhythm, the effortless motion, it was all there, mirrored in the whippet's flight.

Jake crouched instinctively, catching his breath. A smile broke across his face, involuntary and wide.

"That's a fast dog," he said, smiling toward the whippet.

Roberts smiled. "It's a whippet."

Jake crouched lower, letting the whippet sniff his hand. "Makes sense."

"Her name's Dolce," Roberts added. "She's still figuring out how fast she can go."

Dolce looked up.

Roberts tilted his head. "You've got a lot of gears for a soccer player," he said. "You ever run on a clock?"

Jake wiped sweat from his forehead, looking confused. "A clock? Like... for a job?"

Roberts let out a short, dry laugh. "No, son. I mean a stopwatch. Competitive times. You ever had someone measure how fast those legs actually move?"

Jake shrugged. "My school never had a team but I run when I play."

"It's never too late," Roberts replied.

"I'm done with high school anyway. Headed to Springfield next year."

"Springfield?" Roberts repeated, impressed.

"Yeah," Jake said with a small laugh. "Figured I'd see what's out there."

Roberts reached into his jacket and handed him a

card. "If you ever want to find out what that speed can do, give me a call. I'll be expecting it."

Jake took the card, turning it over once before slipping it into his pocket.

From the stands, Paige closed her notebook and stood. She and Jake had grown up on the same street, close enough that his grandmother used to watch her after school when her parents worked late. Their lives had intertwined early. Memories of shared dinners. Long summers that blurred into each other. When they got older, the friendship shifted into something more. By their teens, they were inseparable. Now they were both heading to Springfield.

She had been watching for most of the game, drawn less by the soccer than by how Jake moved. As the man and the dog turned back toward the trail, she stepped closer, catching Jake's eye before smiling.

Paige stepped down from the stands, her notebook tucked under her arm.

"That dog had a heart-shaped mark on its chest. Did you see?" she asked.

Jake shook his head.

She looked toward the trail where the man had disappeared, then at the small white card in Jake's hand.

"You're going to call him," she said.

Jake looked at the card, then back at the soccer field where his friends were packing up.

"I'm thinking about it."

Thinking about it turned into two weeks of restless sleep and a card that grew soft and frayed from being pulled out of his pocket a dozen times a day.

Now, the grass of the park was gone, replaced by the sterile, expensive scent of recycled rubber and fresh white paint. Standing at the edge of the college track, Jake felt the tightness in his chest.

The far wall of the stadium held four large championship banners, their color faded enough to suggest they'd been earned before anyone currently running had arrived. Below them, a row of framed photographs, team shots mostly, but among them individual portraits, Springfield runners who had gone on. Two Olympics. Three national titles in the last decade alone. Jake didn't know the faces yet but he understood what the wall was saying.

The late morning sun glinted off the track, the white lines crisp and perfect against the gleaming red rubber.

Runners moved like a single unit, every stride measured. They all breathed the same way, and it was the type of running that looked slow until you tried to keep up. Jake walked, trying not to make a sound.

He fingered the card from Coach Roberts in his pocket, remembering the man's words from weeks ago at the park: "If you ever want to find out what that speed can do, give me a call."

A whistle pierced the air. Jake hesitated for only a moment before stepping forward. The coach stood near the starting blocks, clipboard in hand, scanning the runners.

"Coach Roberts?" Jake called, his voice catching slightly.

The coach's eyes flicked up, sharp but not unkind. "Yeah?"

”I wanted to introduce myself,” Jake said, holding out the card. “From a few weeks back, you said to reach out if I wanted to join.”

Coach Roberts glanced at the card, then back at the track. “I remember. Alright, walk-on,” he said, voice firm. “See that guy with the clipboard by the hurdles? That's the compliance officer. Tell him I sent you, sign whatever he hands you. Then get changed, anything works, but not a green uniform.” He looked down at Jake's shoes. “Are you running in those?”

Jake glanced at his worn sneakers and grimaced. “Uh… yeah, unless.”

The coach shook his head with a small smirk. “You'll manage. Try not to trip over yourself.”

Jake turned toward the locker room, card still warm in his hand. The smell of sweat and liniment hit him immediately. Uniforms were stacked neatly on benches: green jackets, shorts, socks, perfect, unblemished. He pulled on one of the plain warm-ups from the lockers, snug but unremarkable, and ran a hand down the front anyway, like it might help.

Back on the track, he scanned the group again. The runners in green moved like they'd been running together for years, reading each other without looking. Jake looked at that green and knew he wanted in. But for now, he was stuck with the others like him: plain warm-ups, hesitant eyes, all of them watching, waiting. His stomach sank.

A voice at his side pulled him from his thoughts. “You're a walk-on too?” A boy asked, adjusting his sleeves nervously. His eyes were sharp, assessing.

“Yeah,” Jake replied.

"Good luck holding their line. They're hitting sixty-five-second quarters today, and Roberts pulls anyone who falls off the pack," the boy said, nodding toward the green-uniform runners.

"I'll manage," Jake muttered, more to himself than the boy.

Coach Roberts blew the whistle: "Eight-hundred-meter warm up! I want to see two-minute laps, nothing faster, nothing slower. On my mark!" Jake stepped onto the track. The first footfall was awkward, heavy, wrong. But he pushed forward, one stride at a time, letting the pace of others guide him. The laps blurred. His lungs burned. His calves ached. He was still a walk-on, still outside the circle, still chasing the green.

As Jake slowed near the far curve, a ripple of movement at the edge of the track pulled his attention away.

An entourage had arrived.

They didn't wear spikes or team colors, but they moved with purpose and confidence. Mitch broke from the group mid-stride, laughing as he jogged over. A man followed close behind him, broad-shouldered, sunburned, stopwatch hanging from his neck. Two others lingered nearby, arms crossed, eyes tracking splits.

Jake would learn later that they were Mitch's parents. That both of them had run at the collegiate level. That the others weren't spectators at all, but private coaches, people who had been shaping Mitch's stride and strategy for years before this track had ever mattered.

The man spoke, quietly, firmly, made it sound like instructions, not suggestions. Mitch listened, nodded once, then peeled back onto the track. It was clear this wasn't new. The coach noticed it too. Jake saw Coach Roberts glance over, expression unreadable, before turning back to the whistle in his hand.

Mitch didn't arrive by accident.

He was a five-star recruit. The top middle-distance runner in California. The type of athlete, programs were built around, not brought in through side doors. Springfield had spent twenty years becoming the program that didn't need to chase recruits. It came to them. Coaches from other programs knew the name. The wall in the stadium corridor told the story plainly enough. Two Olympians in the last decade, four All-Americans, a conference record in the 1500 that stood for eleven years. Tom Hughes had flown Mitch out his senior year of high school, walked him through that corridor, let the wall do the talking. By the time they reached Roberts' office, Mitch had decided.

Springfield was his.

Jake stood at the edge of the lane, chest heaving, sweat burning his eyes. He didn't look at the banners or the photographs anymore. He watched the green uniform move down the backstretch, easy and loose while he waited for the whistle to blow again.

Chapter Three

The party was loud when Jake arrived.

Music pulsed through the old sorority house, bass rattling the windows. Strings of lights were hung carelessly between trees. Someone had dragged speakers onto the porch. Someone else had lost a shoe.

Jake stood at the edge of it, hands in his pockets, watching.

It was his first weekend on campus. One practice in. One whistle. One glimpse of what he wasn't part of yet.

Green jackets were everywhere, moving through the crowd with the ease of people who expected to be known. People made space for them without realizing they were doing it.

Jake stayed near the side of the yard with another walk-on, both of them pretending not to listen while Mitch held court near the porch.

"…telling you, last lap I didn't even feel it," Mitch was saying, cup raised, voice carrying. Laughter rippled outward.

Then Paige arrived. Jake noticed before Mitch did.

She stepped through the side gate, denim jacket loose over a white top, hair pulled back enough to show her face. She scanned the yard once, and her eyes landed on Jake.

Mitch kept talking, but his rhythm faltered. His eyes drifted.

Jake felt it immediately. Paige crossed the yard and stopped in front of him. "You look overwhelmed."

He smiled, relieved. "You have no idea." She gestured towards the house. "Come on. It's worse inside, but at least you can't hear yourself think."

They slipped through the door together.

The living room was packed, bodies moving, music louder, heat thick in the air. Someone was dancing on a couch. Someone else was shouting lyrics into a phone.

Jake and Paige danced. Neither danced serious or impressively, but enough to feel part of it. Jake grabbed two cups from the kitchen and handed one to Paige.

She took it and held it. A song later, she set the cup down untouched. "I'm good," she said when Jake raised an eyebrow.

"I was going to grab another."

"Not for me."

He headed back toward the kitchen.

When Jake returned, Mitch was there.

He stood too close to Paige, one arm braced casually against the wall, green jacket open. Another runner hovered nearby, watching.

"So," Mitch was saying, smiling, "you always go for track guys, or am I lucky tonight?"

Paige laughed once. "You're definitely not lucky."

Mitch grinned wider. "Careful. I might take that as a challenge."

"Don't flatter yourself," she said easily. "I'm not interested."

But Mitch didn't move.

Jake stepped in just as Mitch reached out and plucked the drink from Jake's hand.

"Appreciate it," Mitch said, taking a sip. "That's

his," someone said behind him, snickering. "He's a walk-on."

Mitch looked at Jake, then at Paige.

He laughed. "Walk-on," he repeated, like it explained everything. He handed the cup to the guy beside him. "C'mon."

He turned to his friends. "Let's go."

They left the dance floor laughing, green jackets parting the crowd.

Jake stood there, heat rising in his face. Paige touched his arm.

"Hey," she said. "It's nothing." He searched her face. "That didn't look like nothing."

She shrugged, turning away. "He was just talking."

From the doorway, he watched Mitch disappear into the noise.

They left the party together.

The party noise fell behind them and became quieter the longer they walked. Their shoes made a soft sound against the pavement. Paige stopped walking.

Her hand flew to her mouth and she stepped onto the grass, retching. Jake moved.

"Hey…" He put a hand on her back. "Too much to drink?"

She shook her head, still bent forward.

"Paige."

"I didn't drink anything."

She straightened, wiping her mouth with the back of her hand, not looking at him yet.

She lowered herself onto the curb, and he sat beside her. The path lights flickered on one by one down the long stretch of campus walk, each one catching then holding.

She stared at the ground.

"I'm pregnant."

Jake stood up.

He didn't go anywhere. He couldn't sit. He took three steps down the pavement, stopped, ran both hands through his hair, and stood there with his back to her, breathing hard.

"Jake..."

"Just..." he held up a hand. "Give me a second."

She waited.

He turned and looked at her, his face was completely unguarded. Eighteen years old and terrified, the math running behind his eyes in real time. Going to school and running wasn't easy. Concerns about money. His grandmother back home who'd given everything she had to raise him. The future he'd spent two weeks working up the nerve to even reach for, now felt like a forgotten memory.

"I don't." He stopped. Started again. "I don't know how to. We just got here, Paige."

"I know."

"I have nothing. I have literally nothing. My shoes don't match on that track and I'm supposed to."

He stopped himself. Pressed his fingers against his mouth. Looked away.

Paige didn't flinch. She'd braced for this.

He paced once, twice, then sat back down beside her. Not close. His elbow on his knees, staring at the ground between his feet. The silence stretched.

"I'm sorry," he said. "That was... I'm sorry. I needed a second."

"You're allowed a second," she said.

He turned to look at her, really look at her, and whatever was left of the panic shifted. More complicated. More honest.

"Are you okay?" He asked. "Like... are you okay?"

Her face softened at the question.

"I've known for ten days," she said. "I'm past the part where I wasn't."

"Jake." Her voice was quiet but deliberate. "I need to tell you about myself."

He waited.

"My mom raised me alone. Not because she chose to. Because my father made her a promise and then made himself scarce the moment things got hard." She paused. "She never said a bad word about him. She filled every gap herself with whatever she had, her faith, her stubbornness. I watched her do that my whole life." She kept her eyes forward. "I know how it's done. I could do it if I had to."

"But," she said, turning to face him, "I need one thing from you. And I need you to mean it when you say it."

"What?"

"Promise me this child will know its father. Not a name on a form. Not a phone call when it's convenient." Her voice didn't shake, but her eyes were steady, the kind people get when they're working hard to hold it together. "Promise me you won't disappear."

The words sat between them and stayed there.

Jake thought, without meaning to, about his grandmother's kitchen.

Certain things arrive without announcing themselves, settling into the body before the mind has time to prepare.

He was nine, maybe ten. Early enough that the world still felt like it was built around her.

Saturday mornings in her kitchen had a smell, genmaicha tea combined with the sweetness of her banana cinnamon butter cake, still warm in the oven. It was the smell of a place that had absorbed decades of living and stopped apologizing for it.

His grandmother moved through everything, without hurry, without waste. She knew where every pot lived, which burner ran hot, which drawer stuck if you didn't lift the handle slightly before pulling.

Jake sat at the table with his cereal going soft, watching her. He did this most mornings without knowing he was doing it; studying her like you study the things that anchor you, trying to understand what they're made of in case you ever need to build it yourself.

Outside the window, two boys ran past on the sidewalk, their footsteps loud and then gone. Jake watched the empty pavement after they disappeared.

"Grandma."

She made a sound that meant she was listening.

"Did my mom and dad know they were loved?"

He hadn't planned the question. It arrived like important questions usually do, from somewhere below thought. He'd been turning it over for weeks, maybe months. His parents had died when he was four, a car accident on a January highway, black ice, no warning, and he had almost no memories of them. Only photographs.

His grandmother set down what she was holding.

Without ceremony. Not like the question had startled her. She put the bowl on the counter and turned around, giving the question what it deserved, her full attention and the respect of a real answer.

She looked at him. Her face had the quality it always had when she was being precise. Completely present.

"They knew," she said. "Because I told them. Every single day."

Jake stared at his cereal.

He didn't understand the answer. He was nine. He understood the surface of it, that yes, they had been loved, that his grandmother had made certain of it, but underneath, the idea that love was not a feeling you wanted to overcome by, but a decision you made out loud every morning, that was beyond him.

His grandmother turned back to the counter. Picked up the bowl. Kept moving, as if having answered the hardest question in her room she could now return without ceremony to the ordinary work of the day.

Jake finished his cereal. He rinsed his bowl without being asked. He put on his shoes by the back door, sneaker, worn, thin at the toe, shoes that suggested speed even standing still. He went outside to find those boys and whatever they were chasing.

He ran the rest of that morning until the light changed and his grandmother's voice drifted from a window somewhere, calling him home for lunch. He came breathless, grinning, not yet knowing what speed was or what it would someday cost him. Not yet knowing anything except the simple joy of motion and the smell of her kitchen waiting at the end of it.

Now, sitting on a curb in Springfield with Paige beside him, he sat with that memory until something in it unlocked.

"I'm not going to disappear," he said.

She searched his face for the exit ramp, the soft qualification, the hedge. She didn't find one.

"Jake."

"I promise." He held her gaze. "I promise you."

The breath she let out was long and unsteady. She pressed her fingers over her eyes. When she lowered her hand, she reached over and took his.

"Paige," he said. "I love you."

"I should have told you before any of this."

She was quiet. When she answered, her voice was smaller than he'd ever heard it.

"I know," she said, "I love you too."

They sat while the campus settled into stillness around them. Neither moved to go. Above them, the path lights held steady, the long row of them stretching into the dark.

Chapter Four

Campus moved like nothing had happened.

Jake walked to the track with his bag slung over one shoulder, the night before still sitting heavy. Students passed him laughing, talking about classes, parties, people they'd decided mattered. No one knew what he was carrying. No one could see it.

At the track, the green jackets were warming up.

Mitch stood near the inside lane, stretching casually, joking with two other runners. He looked rested and untouched.

Jake took a lane farther out.

Mitch glanced over. "You good?" he called.

Jake grinned. "Yeah."

Coach Roberts blew the whistle.

Warm-up laps.

Jake started easy, but his body didn't listen. His legs surged, then checked themselves. Surge. Ease. The rhythm came out fractured, uneven. A few runners glanced back.

Mitch fell in beside him for half a lap.

"In a hurry?" Mitch asked, not unkindly. Curious.

Jake shrugged. "Gets me there."

Mitch smirked. "Keep going."

He drifted ahead, stride smooth, effortless.

Jake tried to copy it.

During drills, it got worse. On strides, Jake blasted the first fifty meters, then faded hard. On recoveries, he stood bent over, hands on knees, chest heaving while others stayed loose, bouncing lightly.

Roberts watched without saying anything.

Jake felt it all unraveling. Between reps, he sat on the grass and stared at the track. He pictured Paige on the curb. The word she'd said. They had only recently moved in together, a simple apartment in Cottage Grove about a half hour away from campus. Their part time jobs hardly paid for the rent. Now he had more to think about.

Mitch ran past and slowed. "You don't have to kill each rep," he said. "It's not a race."

Jake looked up. "Isn't it?"

Mitch paused, then laughed lightly. "Not yet."

He jogged off.

Practice ended with cooldown laps. Jake lagged behind, form breaking down as he surged one last time for no reason at all, then paid for it.

"Jake," Roberts called.

Jake stopped, bracing himself.

"Stick around," the coach said.

The others drifted away, chatter returning as if practice had never been hard. Mitch walked past Jake, towel over his shoulder.

"See you," he said.

The field emptied. That's when Roberts whistled for Dolce. The little whippet came tearing across the grass.

Roberts tossed the ball and Dolce exploded after it, a blur of white and grey. She hit top speed in three strides, grabbed the ball and trotted back, her tongue lolling out the side of her mouth, chest pumping.

"You see that?" Roberts gestured towards Dolce. "She ran thirty meters in less than 3 seconds. That's a flash."

Jake watched the dog drop and sink, panting hard.

"But look at her now," Roberts said, voice flat. "Tongue sticking out, tank empty. You like to gas out at thirty meters, Jake? Because that's what you're doing out there. It's a 14-15 minute race."

Jake watched. It settled.

"Fast isn't your problem," Roberts said. "You don't know when to stop attacking."

Roberts stayed beside him longer than necessary.

"You don't have to carry everything at once," the coach said, eyes still on Dolce as she circled back. "Running has a way of making the weight feel heavier than it is."

Jake watched attentively.

Roberts finally looked at him. "You thinking about quitting?"

Jake hesitated, then answered honestly. "Yeah."

Roberts didn't flinch. "That doesn't make you weak. It makes you overwhelmed." He paused. "Big difference."

Jake stared at the track. "I don't know how to do all of it."

"You don't," Roberts said. "You do today. Then tomorrow. That's it."

No one spoke.

Roberts clapped Jake lightly on the shoulder.

"Stick with me," he said. "We'll sort the rest out as it comes. My office. Five minutes."

Jake didn't have time to change. He followed the coach toward the brick building at the edge of the stadium.

The office smelled like damp floor mats. On the wall was a faded poster of the 1996 Olympic team, the corners curling with Scotch tape.

Jake stood inside the door, hands loose at his sides, like he was waiting for instructions he was late to follow.

"Sit," Roberts said.

Jake took the chair opposite the desk. The coach didn't sit. He turned to the whiteboard instead, uncapped a marker, and drew a long horizontal line.

"Five thousand," he said, writing 5K at one end. "Your race."

He dotted the line in uneven bursts.

"Tell me what you're doing." Jake watched the dots, clusters, gaps, clusters again. He swallowed. "I go. Hard. Then I back off. Then I go again."

"How long is 'hard'?"

"Until it hurts."

"And 'back off'?"

Jake hesitated. "Until I can breathe."

Roberts capped the marker and finally sat. "That's not strategy. That's survival." Jake nodded.

Roberts uncapped again and redrew the line, this time smooth, with one long, controlled rise. "This is efficiency. Pressure without panic. You don't spike energy like a match and hope it lasts. You burn like a pilot light."

Jake exhaled through his nose. "It feels slower."

"It is," Roberts said. "At first." He added a second line beneath the first, Jake's jagged bursts again. He circled the gaps. "These recoveries? They're theft. You're stealing seconds from later and paying interest."

Jake stared at the board. "I thought surging kept me in it."

"It keeps you alive," Roberts said. "Different thing."

From outside, spikes clicked against rubber, someone finishing drills.

Roberts turned, studied Jake. "What's on your mind?"

Jake opened his mouth. Closed it.

"Not my business," Roberts added. "Unless it's in the way."

Jake looked down at his hands. He could feel his pulse in his thumbs. "It is."

"Paige's pregnant," Jake said.

Roberts leaned back in his chair. "Okay."

Jake blinked. "Okay?"

"That changes some things," Roberts said. "Not who you are."

"I don't know how I'm supposed to, school, running."

"We're not solving your life today," Roberts said. "We're keeping you from breaking it."

He stood, set the marker down, and gestured toward the board again. "This," he tapped the smooth line, "isn't about being less committed. It's about lasting."

Jake bobbed his head.

Roberts opened a drawer, pulled out a folded practice plan, then stopped. "One more thing."

He walked to the locker room door connected to the office and opened it. On the bench sat a green bag.

"Locker room," Roberts said. "Third stall. Try them."

Jake hesitated. "Coach, I."

"I'm tired of seeing you in that gray cotton shirt. Take the team gear. If you can't hit your splits tomorrow, I want it back on my desk." Roberts said.

Inside the bag were spikes, plain, scuffed, nothing flashy and a green singlet folded cleanly beneath.

Jake didn't touch them right away.

"This doesn't change expectations," Roberts said from the doorway. "It raises them."

Jake finally reached out. The fabric was light, almost fragile. He ran his thumb along the seam.

When he came back out, Roberts was writing again, this time a single word under the smooth line.

TIMING.

"Tomorrow," Roberts said, not looking at him. "You run controlled. No theatrics. Let the race come to you."

When the door closed behind Jake, the office went quiet again.

Roberts capped his marker and walked back to his desk, closed the laptop with a gentle push, and opened the top drawer to put away his whistle.

Inside the drawer, tucked under a stack of eligibility

forms, was a family photo of him, his wife and their son. The boy was wearing an oversized Springfield jersey, his face smeared with chocolate ice cream. Roberts touched the corner of the frame, the glass was cracked.

Roberts then glanced towards the door Jake left through. and closed the drawer.

Outside, Mitch jogged past with two other runners, laughing. He glanced over, polite smile in place, then his eyes flicked to the green peeking from Jake's bag.

Chapter Five

The green felt heavier than it looked.

Jake noticed it the moment he stepped onto the track. The fabric pulled at his shoulders, a reminder that whatever he did today would be seen.

Conversations softened as he passed.

Mitch was stretching near lane three, one knee down, arms loose, relaxed in a way that looked earned. He glanced up, eyes flicking to Jake's singlet, then back to his stretch.

"Roberts forgot to lock the equipment room," Mitch said lightly.

A few runners chuckled.

Coach Roberts blew the whistle. "Form up."

They moved through drills, A-skips and short accelerations. Jake shortened his stride, focusing on a midfoot strike to keep from rolling over the heels of the runner in front of him. He forced a low breath and kept his gaze on Mitch's calves.

He ran tall, and held back but it felt wrong.

On the first interval, Mitch floated to the front without effort. Wire to wire. Easy lead. Jake tucked in behind, legs itching. The old habit whispered: go now.

By the third repeat, his lungs burned in a new way,

less panic, more pressure. He wasn't gasping. He was holding.

Mitch glanced back once.

During recovery, Jake jogged instead of stopping. Dolce's blur flashed through his mind.

"Different look," Mitch said as they lined up again. "You get new advice?"

Jake shrugged. "Trying."

"Careful," Mitch said, still smiling. "5K's don't forgive patience."

The next rep started fast. Mitch pushed the pace early, daring someone to come with him. Jake felt it, the invitation, the trap. He let Mitch have the front, settled off his shoulder.

Jake noticed Mitch's lead foot landing a fraction too far forward, he was working too hard to stay easy.

They finished the set. Jake crossed the line breathing hard but intact. Mitch slowed, hands on hips, sweat darkening the collar of his singlet.

Roberts said nothing, only watched.

After practice, the locker room hummed. Laughter. Music from someone's phone. Jake changed quickly, still unsure where he fit.

Mitch bumped his shoulder as he passed. "Nice pacing today Jake. Keep that up and I might actually add you to the team photo," he said.

Outside, Jake sat on the bleachers tying his shoes again, even though they were tight.

Roberts joined him, hands in his pockets. "How'd it feel?"

"Like I was holding back," Jake said.

"You were, but you're maintaining reserves for later in the race."

Jake looked out at the track. "Mitch keeps going early."

"He always has," Roberts said. "Wire to wire works until it doesn't."

Jake thought of the board. The smooth line. "What if I miss my chance?"

Roberts studied him. "You won't. You'll recognize it."

Jake asked, "And if I don't?"

"Then you learn," Roberts said. "And you don't break."

As Roberts walked away, Jake stayed seated a moment longer. He pressed his palms into his thighs.

Across the field, Mitch laughed with two teammates, already recovered.

Marc Cianfarani

Chapter Six

The bus ride to the meet was louder than practices were. Music leaked from cheap headphones. Someone joked about lane assignments. Someone else pretended not to care.

Jake sat by the window, knees bouncing. A dull heat gathered under his ribs, not pain, but that tight pressure. He pressed his hand to his stomach once, casually, hoping nobody noticed. The closer they got, the worse the hollow feeling got, that faint rising nausea he remembered he'd get.

Up front, Mitch and two scoring seniors occupied the "power seats," their legs stretched into the aisle. Outside, the valley floor ran flat and wide in both directions. Filbert orchards lined the highway in long even rows, the branches still holding the last of their leaves. Further out, grass seed fields stretched pale and unharvested toward the tree line.

To the west the Coast Range sat low against the sky, the grey-blue that in Oregon didn't mean far away, but permanent. A water tower appeared briefly with a town name he didn't catch. Then the first billboard for the meet.

Watching farmland blur into bleachers and

banners, Jake told himself it was another run. Only distance and pace. His chest wouldn't settle.

Coach Roberts walked the aisle once, checking shoes, nodding. He stopped beside Jake.

"Same thing," Roberts said. "Nothing new today."

Jake dipped his chin.

The track was fast, tight turns, fresh rubber. Mitch warmed up with two teammates, loose in the shoulders like the outcome was settled.

Jake warmed up on the infield, trying not to watch him. His strides still looked a half-beat awkward, too much reach, not enough patience. He heard Coach Roberts behind him.

"Easy," the coach said, "you're not proving anything in warmup."

His legs felt fine, but his breathing didn't.

He tried for a long inhale and got halfway there, his breathing too quick and too shallow. Around him other runners went through their routines, tapping their spikes, rolling their shoulders, shaking out arms with practiced calm. Jake copied the motions, but they felt borrowed, like someone else's warmup.

His hands weren't steady. He pressed them into his hamstrings and held the stretch longer than he needed to.

They called the event. The hush fell, that strange, collective pause before effort. He could still feel his pulse in the tips of his fingers. He glanced once toward Mitch. Mitch didn't look back.

The gun cracked.

Jake came out controlled, cautious. The field surged. Mitch went straight to the front, clean and confident, making it clear this was his race.

Jake didn't settle; he jammed himself into the pocket Roberts had assigned, staring at the twitch of Mitch's calves

Mitch was a metronome at the front, pulling the entire pack into a pace that felt like a slow suffocation. Jake stayed on the rail, taking elbows from runners.

Halfway through, instinct whispered: Go now, but he didn't. Instead, he remembered the field. Dolce. The word timing.

With two laps to go, the race tightened. Mitch quickened. Jake responded, not a surge, but presence. He was there, and the gap didn't widen.

On the final bend, Jake finally let it open. His stride stretched, cleaner than it had ever felt. He moved past one runner, then another, but the leaders were gone.

He crossed the line mid-pack. Sixth. Maybe seventh.

He bent over, hands on knees, lungs burning. The leaders were walking it off, chest still heaving but upright.

Two hundred meters. Maybe two-fifty.

That was the gap. Distance that had existed, before the gun fired and would exist again next time unless changes were made in the space between now and then.

Part of him wanted to believe he could have caught them. That if the surge had come fifty meters earlier, if he'd trusted the pace instead of checking it, the gap would have closed. He turned the race over once, looking for the seam where it came apart.

He couldn't find one.

"You ran it right," Roberts said.

"Thanks."

Across the track, Mitch crossed cleanly, controlled to the end.

As Mitch slowed, he finally glanced over at Jake.

On the ride home, the bus was quieter.

Jake stared out the window again, replaying the laps.

The first race didn't change Jake's place on the team.

The green jackets kept their hierarchy, and Mitch stayed exactly where he had always been, at the front, untouched.

That freshman year increments were small. A second shaved here. A place gained there. He learned how to finish races without folding, how to hold form when his lungs screamed. He learned when not to go. He didn't win. He didn't medal.

Mitch, meanwhile, broke records with school firsts and state attention.

Jake watched and trained and went home tired.

That summer, Emily was born.

Chapter Seven

Jake pushed through the apartment door, a plastic bag swinging from his hand.

"I got it," he said, smiling. "Strawberry. The place on Alde still had some."

Paige didn't look up.

"Forget the ice cream."

He stopped.

"What?"

Another contraction hit. She gripped the back of the kitchen chair, eyes closing.

"I don't want it," she said, breath tight. "I'm having contractions."

The smile dropped off his face.

"Oh…" He set the bag down too fast. "Oh shit."

He stepped toward her, hands half raised.

"Okay, okay. Breathe. Like they taught us. In through your nose, out through your mouth. Look at me."

She followed it once. In. Out.

Then she opened her eyes.

"Jake."

"Yeah."

"Fuck off."

He stopped.

He stood there, hands still lifted, like he wasn't sure where to put them.

"Okay," he said.

Another contraction came. She turned away from him and gripped the counter this time.

He stayed where he was.

The ice cream softened in the bag by the door.

Jake moved toward the cabinet, then stopped halfway.

"Hold on," he said.

Paige didn't answer.

He had his phone out.

"What am I looking for?" he muttered. "Contractions… timing… how far apart…"

He scrolled too fast, eyes searching for anything useful.

"They said in the class…"

"Jake."

"I want to make sure we're not going too early again."

"Jake."

He looked up.

She was watching him now, one hand still braced against the counter.

"Put the phone away," she said.

He hesitated.

"We should go."

That landed.

He slipped the phone into his pocket.

"Okay."

Paige shifted, then went still.

"Wait."

Jake froze.

"What?"

She frowned slightly, looking down and then back up.

"I think something… happened."

"What do you mean?"

"I don't know." She shook her head once. "It felt like something."

That was enough.

Jake grabbed the hospital bag beside the table, nearly missing the strap the first time.

"Okay," he said. "We're going."

The drive there felt too short and too long at the same time. Jake kept both hands locked on the wheel and checked the dashboard clock every thirty seconds as if time might start behaving differently if he stared at it hard enough. Paige sat angled toward the window, one hand resting against the curve of her stomach, breathing through what came when it came.

He glanced over at a red light.

"How far apart?"

"I'm not timing them."

"You should probably time them."

She turned her head and looked at him.

"Drive."

He drove.

At the hospital entrance he was out of the car before the engine had fully settled. He came around too fast, opened her door, reached for the bag, then the door to the building, then seemed to realize he only had two hands. Paige got out on her own and walked past him, one hand pressed to her lower back.

Inside, the lights were too bright. The waiting room television was on mute. Somewhere down the hall a baby cried, then stopped.

A nurse in pale blue scrubs took them in, calm like someone who had seen every version of panic and no longer borrowed any of it.

Paige answered the questions. Jake stood beside her with the bag in one hand and his wallet in the other.

The nurse came back.

"It's not your water," she said. "It happens. It can feel that way. Everything's moving in the right direction. But not yet."

Paige nodded.

Jake nodded too quickly.

The nurse gave him a brief look that wasn't unkind.

"Go home," she said. "Try to rest. When it's time, you'll know."

Outside, the night had gone colder.

Jake started the car and pulled out of the lot. Neither of them said anything. Streetlights slid across the windshield in slow intervals. The roads were mostly empty.

"You said it felt different," Jake said finally.

"It did."

"They said it wasn't."

Paige kept her eyes on the window.

A few seconds passed.

"I don't want to get it wrong," he said.

"You're not the one getting it wrong," she said.

He tightened the grip on the wheel slightly, then loosened it again.

They drove another block in silence.

Paige shifted in her seat.

Then she went still.

"Jake."

He didn't look over right away.

"What?"

"Pull over."

He turned.

"This isn't the same," she said.

He slowed the car.

"You're sure?"

She nodded once.

"Yes."

Another second passed.

Then she looked down, then back at him

"My water broke."

This time he believed her.

"Okay."

He turned the car around.

Neither of them said anything after that.

The streets were quieter now. Fewer lights. Fewer cars. Jake drove faster than before, not recklessly, without the hesitation from earlier. Paige sat still beside him, one hand braced lightly against the seat, her breathing steady when it could be, controlled when it couldn't.

Another contraction came.

She closed her eyes and let it move through her.

Jake glanced over, then back to the road.
"You okay?"
"Yes."
"This is it," she said.
He tightened his grip on the wheel.
"Okay."
The hospital came into view, all white light and glass.

Chapter Eight

The hospital smell hit him before the doors finished opening.

Jake had been awake for nineteen hours. He knew because he'd watched each one pass from the plastic chair beside Paige's bed, tracking time like he'd tracked splits. Methodically. Helplessly.

She hadn't complained. She moved through it, jaw set, eyes focused.

He held her hand and felt useless in the way that men do in rooms where women are doing all the work.

Nurses came and went and machines beeped. Outside the narrow window, the sky went from dark to pale to a grey-white Oregon morning that wasn't going to get any brighter.

Roberts had texted once. *Thinking of you both. Take the time you need.*

Jake had stared at it before setting his phone face down on the chair.

She arrived at 6:12 in the morning, red-faced and furious about being asked to exit.

Jake stood at the edge of the room and felt the floor shift.

His knees softened, and he pressed one hand flat

against the wall to steady himself.

Later, when the room had quieted and the light through the window had warmed, a nurse appeared with a clipboard and a kind, efficient smile.

"Have you decided on a name?"

Jake opened his mouth.

"We didn't."

"Emily," Paige said it. Clearly. Like you say it if you've known for a long time.

Jake turned.

She was looking at the baby, like she hadn't stopped since they'd placed her in her arms. Her voice had been quiet, but there was nothing uncertain in it.

Emily.

His mother's name. The name that had lived for years in a space he'd kept mostly closed, tucked somewhere between his grandmother's kitchen and the parts of his childhood he didn't take out often.

He hadn't told Paige. He was almost certain he hadn't told her.

He looked at Paige. She still hadn't looked up.

He looked back at the baby.

At Emily.

Her eyes closed, her mouth working slightly at nothing, her small fist pressed against her cheek as if she were thinking through. She had no idea what her name was. She had simply arrived.

"Emily," Jake said.

Paige looked up then, and found his face and went still. She read it immediately, as she always had. She didn't say anything. She held his gaze, and waited.

Jake crossed the room.

He looked down at his daughter, the small, certain, new person who already had his mother's name and Paige's composure.

He looked at Paige.

"You're incredible," he said.

Paige exhaled, pressing her lips together.

Outside, the city was moving, buses and early footsteps and the distant rhythm of a world that didn't know or care what had happened in room 114. But inside, the three of them were still.

Emily's fist opened and closed against nothing.

When he held her the first time, her fingers closed around his thumb with a grip that surprised him, firm and certain, like she knew what she wanted to hold onto.

The nights were long. Sleep came in pieces. When she cried he would rock her, and he walked the apartment with her against his chest, pacing slow circles in the dark, singing You Are My Sunshine under his breath until the words thinned into melody and her breathing finally evened out against his collarbone.

Running changed. It stopped being escape and became structure, the thing that held the rest of his days.

He ran early, before work, in the grey, pre-dawn when the streets belonged only to him and the occasional dog walker. He ran late, after Emily slept, his breath clouding in the cold air, the apartment window glowing faint and warm behind him as he went. Some days his legs felt hollow. Other days they felt unbreakable. He stopped questioning either.

By the time sophomore year ended, life had

narrowed.

Emily was a year old. She walked unsteadily, listing slightly to the left, correcting herself with a focus that made him laugh every time. When he came through the door, she reached for him with both hands, not one, always both as if one might not be enough to pull him all the way in.

Paige worked evenings. Jake picked up whatever shifts he could find. Training fit into the leftover spaces, the margins of days that didn't have much margin. Early mornings. Late nights. Miles run on borrowed time with borrowed energy, fueled mostly by coffee.

When junior year began, Jake returned to the track leaner and quieter and more exact.

The freshman who had surged and faded again was gone.

He no longer showed up to prove anything.

The results followed in increments, like real things do.

He placed fourth at the first meet of junior year, then fifth which felt like regression until Roberts reminded him it wasn't… then third.

He stood on the edge of the results board after that one and looked at his name before walking away.

Still no win.

Mitch continued to win. Cleanly, publicly, bigger crowds, louder applause, his name spoken in the tone reserved for people whose outcomes feel inevitable. Jake heard it in locker rooms, on buses, in how coaches from visiting teams looked past everyone else when they scanned the field.

He felt none of the old heat rise in him.

At the final meet of junior year, Jake placed second.

He crossed and stood bent over, hands on his knees, letting the race settle.

When he straightened, he found Paige at the fence.

She stood with Emily balanced on her hip, one hand raised to shade her eyes against the afternoon sun. Emily had no idea what a race was or why people were clapping or what any of this meant. She clapped anyway, enthusiastically, her whole small body involved in it.

Jake walked over.

He was still breathing hard, still sweat-soaked, still somewhere between the race and the world on the other side of it. He reached over the fence, lifted Emily, and held her against his chest without caring about the sweat or heat or her fist tightening in the singlet.

She kept clapping against his shoulder.

He laughed.

Across the track, Mitch broke the tape. The applause sharpened.

Of course.

After the race, Mitch found him near the fence.

He was relaxed, loose, like someone for whom finishing first required no recovery. He clapped Jake on the shoulder, said the right things, clean and practiced. Then his eyes drifted, to Paige.

"You're looking good."

Paige smiled thinly. "Thanks."

Jake noticed and said nothing.

He lifted Emily a little higher on his chest and turned slightly, not dramatically and not with anger. A quiet redrawing of the boundary. Emily grabbed his ear and he let her.

Mitch moved on.

That summer was the best one.

Jake trained harder than he ever had. He felt a certain rightness. Like the life he was living and the running he was doing had finally stopped pulling against each other and started moving in the same direction.

Emily came with him on cooldowns, riding his shoulders with her hands tangled in his hair, squealing when he picked up pace, which made him pick up the pace more, which made her squeal louder. He pushed the stroller between intervals, lungs, burning, the wheels chattering over uneven pavement, and when she laughed at nothing, at the wind or motion or some private joke only she understood, laughter spilled out of him too.

One afternoon in late August, warm and unhurried, Emily tugged at his shirt from the stroller.

He looked down.

She was looking up at him with the gravity of a small person about to say something important. Her mouth worked once, twice.

"Daddy," she said.

Then with great effort and enormous pride:

"Up."

She beamed.

Jake crouched in front of her.

"Did you..."

"Daddy Up," Paige said from the bench behind him, laughing softly.

"Are you trying to say Daddy Up, honey?"

Emily looked between them, pleased with the response she'd generated.

"Daddy Up," she said again, more confident this time.

"Daddy Up!" Jake and Paige said together, without planning to.

Emily shrieked with delight.

Jake lifted her out of the stroller and onto his shoulder, and she squealed all the way up, grabbing his hair, crowing at the height of it, at being held that high by someone who wasn't going to drop her.

He walked three slow circles of the park path like that. Her hands in his hair. Her laughter above him. The late-summer light coming sideways through the trees.

Marc Cianfarani

Chapter Nine

The late-summer air was warm and still as Jake, Paige, and Emily crossed the quiet parking lot toward the stadium. It didn't feel like a race morning yet, no noise, no crowds, but the soft bounce of Emily's steps as she held Jake's finger and toddled beside him.

Roberts was waiting near the entrance, leaning casually against the railing with his arms loosely crossed. He looked more like someone enjoying the morning than a coach gearing up for an event.

Emily spotted him immediately and broke into a huge smile, letting go of Jake's hand so she could wave with both arms at once.

Roberts grinned. "There she is. My favorite part of race day."

"Hi, Coach, hope you had a nice break," said Paige while smoothing Emily's shirt as the little girl clung to Jake's leg.

"She's getting big," replied Roberts.

Jake rolled his shoulders. "Feels strange seeing you calm before a race."

Roberts shrugged lightly. "I'm here early. That's all. You looked tense walking up, so I figured I'd meet you outside."

Paige nudged him. "He was up early. Very early."

Jake sighed. "Don't start."

Paige and Roberts raised matching eyebrows at him.

"Unreal," Jake muttered.

Roberts nodded toward the stadium entrance. "You'll settle once you're changed. Pre-race nerves mean you're alive."

Jake looked around the lot. "Any sign of Mitch?"

Roberts shook his head. "No. He's not coming. He's with his family in France. Their flight got delayed or cancelled. They won't be back till tonight. "

"He'd hate missing this."

"He would," Roberts said. "But today's your race. Focus on that."

Emily reached up toward Jake again, smiling wide, wanting to be picked up. Jake lifted her onto his hip, and she rested her head against his shoulder, still waving one hand toward the stadium like she understood the moment.

Paige touched Jake's arm. "We'll be right here."

Roberts gave Jake a quiet, confident thumbs up.

"Go get changed. We will see you when you come out."

Jake walked out of the tunnel, and the stadium hit him at once, rubber, heat, crowd noise. He found Paige in the stands without trying. Emily was on her hip, both arms in the air. Roberts stood next to them, hands in his pockets.

Jake turned away and got to work. A few strides. Laces. Neck.

The starter called them up.

He took a spot in the middle of the line. Outside enough to see, inside enough to move. The gun fired, and the field lurched forward in a tangle of elbows. Jake let them go. He settled into the second group and watched the front runners spend themselves on the first lap.

He kept his breathing quiet.

At 1200 meters he tucked behind a long-striding guy from the west coast, predictable cadence, reliable anchor and stayed there.

The race thinned, gradually, then obviously. Shoulders dropped around him. Breathing got ragged ahead of schedule. Jake moved through gaps while they opened and didn't chase the ones that didn't.

At 2K, the leader tested the field with a short surge. Half the pack bit. Jake watched them go and held his pace. Two of them were back beside him by 3K, blown, and he slid past without ceremony.

Each time he came through the homestretch he caught Paige and Roberts at the rail. Emily had both fists up.

With 800 to go, the leader pushed again, harder this time. Jake moved with him, close enough to hear the breathing start to crack. He stayed behind him and waited.

The bell rang.

Jake went wide and opened his stride. He came past the leader like the race had been arranged that way. The guy tried to answer, Jake felt the attempt in the air behind him, and then he didn't.

He powered through the curve, arms low, feet quick, and the homestretch came up wide and loud and he drove through the line.

He bent over, hands on knees, breathing hard but not desperate. He knew before he looked up.

Emily was fighting her way out of Paige's arms. Paige reached him first, her arm around his waist, Emily grabbing his face with both hands like she needed to confirm he was real.

Roberts stopped a step back from the rest of it.

"Patient when you needed to be," he said. "Aggressive when it counted."

Jake bowed, still catching his breath.

"National coaches were here," Roberts said. "If they weren't watching that, they weren't doing theirs."

Jake stood with Paige's hand on his back and Emily's fingers at his ear.

He stared at the lane where Mitch would have been and didn't know whether he was glad or disappointed.

He wondered what it would've taken to beat him today.

The next day his legs were heavy.

The trail was quiet like late afternoons get, peaceful, and emptied out. Jake pushed Emily's stroller along the asphalt path, the wheels crunching in a steady rhythm. She kicked her feet against the footrest and watched the trees like she was expecting company.

She wasn't wrong.

Dolce came first, cutting between the trunks in a low white and brindle streak. Roberts followed, hands in his pockets, moving like a man who had nowhere better to be.

Emily threw her arms up. Jake unclipped her before

she could demand it twice and set her down. She walked straight to the dog, both arms out. Dolce dropped her head and held still while the toddler wrapped herself around her neck. She took it.

"Do-she, Do-she," Emily said.

"You know, coach." Jake said, watching the dog's ribs expand and contract with every breath, "I don't think I ever asked. Where'd the name come from?"

Roberts let out a short, dry huff that might have been a laugh. "Spent a summer in Italy when I was twenty. Mostly eating my weight in those little pastries, they sell on every corner. They call them dolce…sweets."

He looked at the brindle whippet, who was currently letting a toddler use her as a pillow.

"She was the only one in the litter that didn't try to take a chunk out of my hand. Seemed like the right fit."

"Sweet!" Jake added laughing.

"The other choice was to name her heart," the coach continued. "Every time, I take her for a walk someone points out that heart shape."

Emily tired of the hug on her own schedule, and Jake lifted her back into the stroller. Dolce fell in beside her like she'd been assigned.

They walked.

"You going to tell me that wasn't your best race?" Roberts asked.

"I stayed controlled."

"You dictated the whole thing. Don't pretend that's nothing."

Jake looked at the path. "Mitch wasn't there."

Roberts stopped long enough that Jake had to look

up.

"The clock doesn't know that," he said. "Neither do the decisions you made."

A soccer ball rolled across the trail. Jake redirected it with a clean touch, sending it back to two kids who tore after it down the hill.

Roberts watched them go. "I found one athlete on this trail. Maybe there's another."

"Those kids would destroy me in a sprint."

"That's not your race." Roberts paused. "And Mitch's shadow isn't either."

They walked for a bit before Roberts spoke again.

"In thirty years, I've never coached two runners in the same event at the same level. Not once." He glanced at Jake.

"You and Mitch are it. On any given day it could go either way."

Jake let that land. Didn't argue it.

"How long have you been coaching?" he asked.

Roberts exhaled a short laugh. "Long enough that I should probably lie about it."

"Did you run?"

"Not like you. But yeah." Roberts took a deep breath. "I got my teaching degree, took the job at the school. That's where I met Mia."

Jake didn't rush him.

"She passed a few years ago."

"Coach…I'm sorry."

Roberts nodded once. Dolce brushed against his leg; he put a hand on her without looking down.

"I have a son. Florida. Real Estate," he said it like it

explained everything. "When Mia got sick, I kept coaching, kept traveling. Thought routine would hold things together."

They kept walking.

"I was driving back from a meet when she died."

Jake stopped pushing.

"I didn't know," Roberts said. "I wasn't there." His eyes stayed on the trail. "My son hasn't forgiven me. Can't say I blame him."

Emily reached out from the stroller and touched Robert's hand. He looked down at her. His face shifted, not a smile, but close.

"You show up," Jake said. "You didn't have to. But you still do."

Roberts didn't answer right away. When he did, his voice was softer.

"Yeah," he said. "Maybe I needed this more than I let on."

The sun stretched long across the path. Dolce stayed beside the stroller. Emily watched her with heavy eyes, almost asleep.

Chapter Ten

Music came through the speaker on the counter, with enough beat that Emily had decided it was for her.

Jake grabbed Emily and swung her onto his shoulders in one motion. She shrieked and grabbed two fistfuls of his hair, holding on while he jogged laps around the apartment. In the kitchen, the pasta lid rattled against the pot. Paige watched from the counter and didn't bother hiding the smile.

"Careful, Em. Dad's going to get tired."

Emily shook her head so hard she nearly unseated herself. "No tired!"

"Right," Paige said. "Not tired. Never tired. Fastest man alive and also Superman."

Emily slapped both palms against the top of Jake's head in agreement.

He laughed, full loud, no filter. He lowered her, spun her once, and set her down. She looked up at him immediately.

"Daddy up?" A question she knew the answer to.

He picked her back up.

They went another few laps before he finally dropped onto the couch, Emily curled against his chest, both of them warm and breathing. She was still moving, half-dancing even while sitting still. Paige hummed in the kitchen. The pasta boiled.

His phone buzzed.

"Who is it?" Paige asked.

"Mitch."

She looked over. "What does he want?"

"Says he's back."

She went back to the counter. Jake typed.

MITCH: Congrats. Lucky I wasn't there.

JAKE: We'll see.

MITCH: You been training all summer?

Emily patted his jaw. He let her.

JAKE: You'll find out.

MITCH: Saw the time. Decent. Enjoy the plastic trophy.

JAKE: The clock didn't ask where you were.

MITCH: Can't wait to show you your place.

Jake read it once. Then again.

JAKE: Why wait?

MITCH: Why wait.

He put the phone down. Emily had lost interest and was watching the kitchen like the pasta was personally for her. Paige set plates on the counter. The music kept going.

Jake sat there still feeling the race in his legs.

After dinner the apartment had gone still.

Paige had finished cleaning up the kitchen and disappeared down the hall with a towel over her shoulder. Emily finally crashed, limbs heavy, her tiny breaths settling into the soft rhythm of sleep in her crib.

The music had stopped.

The pasta smell lingered in the air.

Jake sat on the couch with the lights low, legs stretched out, soreness settling in.

His phone buzzed again.

He checked it without thinking.

It was still Mitch.

MITCH: You up?

No punctuation. No explanation.

Jake leaned his head back against the couch.

JAKE: Yeah.

MITCH: You want to find out early?

Jake stared at the words. He knew exactly what Mitch meant.

JAKE: Trying to lose the rest of your summer?

A pause.

Longer this time.

MITCH: Track at 2?

Jake exhaled.

JAKE: You serious?

MITCH: Always been.

Jake sat there with the phone resting against his thigh. He still felt the excitement of winning. He glanced down the hall. Paige's shadow moved faintly under the doorframe as she folded laundry.

He looked back at the phone.

JAKE: I'll be there.

Jake set the phone face-down on the couch cushion and picked up his shoes.

The track lights were off.

Jake pulled into the empty lot and killed the engine.

He stepped out. The gravel under his feet sounded

too loud.

At the far end of the track, a figure jogged a slow line down the backstretch.

Jake walked toward the infield gate. Mitch saw him.

"You came," Mitch said.

"You asked," Jake answered.

They stood in lane one.

"How far?" Jake asked.

Mitch shrugged. "Two laps. Fast enough to matter."

Jake nodded. "Fine."

They moved to the start line.

"On you," Mitch said.

Jake inhaled once, slow.

"Ready," he said.

They went, not a sprint but a pace below redline. Mitch moved to Jake's shoulder immediately, close enough that Jake felt the heat off him.

In the dark the turns felt sharper. The first hundred meters settled like that. A quiet track with no crowd, no noise except the wind moving across the empty bleachers.

Mitch surged first.

Jake responded, precise rather than panicked. He slid into Mitch's slipstream, breathing through his nose, elbows tight.

At two hundred, the pace sharpened.

At three hundred, neither of them was thinking about practice anymore.

Final lap, Mitch accelerated again, not a full move, enough to make Jake choose. Jake matched it.

At six hundred meters, Mitch drifted out half a lane. An invitation. Or a dare.

Jake took it, and he came up alongside, stride opening, breathing steady. They were even.

Mitch grinned, and then he pushed.

Jake went with him, but felt a sudden tightness in the left leg that shouldn't have been there. He kept running. Didn't break form, but he didn't touch it.

Mitch pulled ahead by a stride. Then another.

Jake held the pace but couldn't close it.

Mitch hit the line first with a sharp exhale.

Jake crossed a second later. He didn't bend over. Didn't gasp.

Mitch walked a slow circle, then came back.

"Not bad," he said, breathing hard. "You're closer than last year."

"Closer than you think," Jake said.

The parking lot was dead except for the ticking of the cooling engines. Mitch popped the trunk of his convertible and pulled out two beers, handing one toward Jake without ceremony.

Jake hesitated for half a second, then took it.

They leaned against the side of the car, sweat cooling in the night air. The track behind them was dark.

Jake cracked his beer. "So…France. You're going to pretend you didn't train at all?"

Mitch snorted. "France? Man, France was…" He shook his head, searching for the right word." Stupid. Beautiful. "

Jake waited.

"My dad had me in a lab in Monaco. Altitude tents and some German tech that measures the lactate in your body every thirty seconds." Jake rolled his eyes. "They had me on a treadmill with a mask on until I puked, then told me my "'ceiling' was higher than it was last year. It wasn't a vacation Jake."

Jake took a drink, watching him over the rim of the bottle.

"But," Mitch said, grinning, "we flew into Nice. And I wasn't supposed to, but I snuck out."

"Of course you did."

"Ran the pier with some dudes from a club team. Whole thing's lit up at night, boardwalk, water, bars spilling music everywhere. You'd love it."

Jake raised a brow. "The running or the bars."

"Both," Mitch said without hesitation. Then smirking, "the rest of it, maybe you wouldn't love."

Jake lifted his bottle. "High-performance fuel."

"Exactly," Mitch said, tapping his bottle against Jake's.

Mitch nudged a pebble with his shoe. "You ran good tonight."

"You too."

They finished their beers.

Mitch tossed his empty into the back seat. "Season's here man. Whatever this was tonight doesn't count; the real stuff starts Friday."

Mitch slid into the driver's seat, engine turning over in a low growl. "Get some sleep. You'll need it."

He drove off.

Chapter Eleven

The weight room opened at six.

Jake was there at five fifty-five, bag on his shoulder, breath still visible in the corridor.

The janitor unlocked the door without looking at him.

The fluorescent light stuttered in sections.

He dropped his bag by the cable station near the far wall.

The room smelled like chalk and rubber.

A few plates sat abandoned on a bar somebody hadn't returned to the rack.

The mirrors ran the full length of the east wall, floor to ceiling.

Jake adjusted the pin on the cable stack and started pulling, twelve reps, controlled, nothing that would wreck him before Friday.

Mitch arrived at six seventeen.

Jake knew without looking.

He heard him, bag dropped.

Mitch set up the cable flies, light weight, high reps.

They worked on opposite ends of the room.

Nobody watching.

The room filled briefly, throwers, a relay sprinter, a pair of hurlers who came in loud and then left.

After a short time, it was the two of them.

And then, without either of them deciding anything, the distance between them began to close.

Mitch moved to the dumbbell rack.

Jake had been at the squat station on that side.

The rack was free.

He loaded the bar and went down slow.

Mitch finished his set and shifted to the bench station four meters away.

Jake squatted again. Three sets.

The distance between them stayed constant.

Then Mitch drifted to the pull-down bar, which happened to be closer.

Jake moved to the seated row, which happened to be closer still.

By seven they were at the dumbbell rack at the same time.

Jake reached for the forties.

Mitch's hand arrived at the same tier a half second later. Closing around the forty-fives.

They both straightened without acknowledging it.

Two men holding dumbbells they may not have needed, standing close enough that the mirror showed them in the same frame.

Jake looked at his own reflection.

Then without meaning to, at Mitch's.

Mitch noticed and said nothing.

He carried his dumbbells to the bench and started

curling, and Jake carried his to the adjacent station and did the same, and the distance between them was now close enough that they could have had a conversation at normal volume if either of them had decided to have one.

Mitch added weight first.

Stood, replaced the dumbbells with a solid crank, selected the next pair up.

Jake watched this in the mirror.

He finished his set.

Selected next pair up.

Jake set the weights down and rolled his shoulders.

He crossed to the mats along the south wall, sat and began to stretch. Hip flexors, hamstrings.

He worked through it methodically.

Then he moved to the floor, planted his palms, and started pushups.

Twenty, clean and controlled, each one full range, chest to the mat, arms locking out at the top. He counted them quietly to himself, finished the set, and sat back on his heels.

In the mirror he could see Mitch watching.

Mitch had a smirk.

Then Mitch sat down what he was holding, crossed the room, and lowered himself to the mat a few feet away.

He set his hands and waited. Jake looked at him. Mitch looked at the floor.

Jake settled back into position.

They started at the same time.

One. Two.

The rhythm matched without either of them finding it deliberately, like two runners falling into stride without agreeing to.

Ten.

Fifteen.

Jake's breathing was steady.

Eyes down.

Each rep exact.

Perfect form.

Mitch kept counting.

Twenty-one. Twenty-two.

Somewhere around twenty-three, Mitch's range of motion negotiated itself. The elbows didn't quite track the same way. The chest didn't reach the same distance from the floor. He was in a pushup position, almost.

Twenty-five.

Jake's eyes were down.

His form was the same it had been on rep one.

Shoulders level.

Core tight.

Twenty-nine. Thirty. Jake slowed.

Thirty-one.

He glanced up.

He looked at Mitch.

Mitch was perhaps four inches off the floor, arms at a comfortable angle, doing a movement that had by this point become its own entirely original exercise.

Jake stopped.

He stared.

Mitch met his eyes.

And then Mitch's face broke open, not gradually, all at once, and he pointed directly at Jake and laughed, loud, unguarded, from the chest.

He rolled onto his side and kept laughing, one hand still pointing.

Jake sat up.

He looked back at Mitch, still pointing laughing, tears starting at the corners of his eyes.

And then Jake started laughing too, the sound surprised out of him.

"You were barely moving," Jake said.

Mitch couldn't answer. He waved a hand vaguely in Jake's direction, which was his best attempt at a response.

"You were doing…" Jake tried again, then lost himself.

They sat on the mat, both of them useless, the weight room empty around them.

Mitch finally got himself under control.

He wiped his eyes with the back of his hand.

He looked at Jake.

"You kept going," he said.

"I didn't know you'd stopped," Jake said.

"I didn't stop," Mitch said. "I adapted."

Jake shook his head.

Mitch lay flat on his back on the mat, staring at the ceiling, still catching his breath from laughing.

"Thirty-one," he said.

"Thirty-one," Jake agreed.

The door at the far end of the corridor banged.

Someone else arriving.

Roberts walked in at seven twenty-two with a clipboard and a coffee.

He checked the corkboard, made a notation, capped his pen and then turned.

Two of his best runners were lying on the mat in the middle of the weight room, staring at the ceiling and doing nothing.

He looked at them.

"Friday," he said, to neither of them specifically.

Chapter Twelve

When senior year opened, the home track was full.

Mitch's parents sat near the finish line. Paige stood with Emily tucked against her chest. The gun fired.

This time, Jake didn't fade. He waited, moved when it mattered and crossed first.

Mitch slowed behind him, jaw tight. His father reached Jake first, smiling wide, hand extended.

"You ran a hell of a race," he said. "You should come by for dinner sometime."

Jake nodded, still catching his breath.

Emily broke free from Paige and ran toward him, shouting, "Daddy! Daddy!"

Jake crouched as she collided into him, wrapping her arms around his neck. He lifted her easily, her excitement buzzing against his chest.

Paige reached them a moment later, pulling him into an embrace around Emily.

"You did it," she whispered.

The world had become the small circle of Emily's arms around his neck and Paige's hand on his shoulder, the noise of the bleachers fading into the background.

Paige shifted Emily onto her other side and looked toward the fence. Mitch's father stood with his back mostly turned, voice low, one hand on Mitch's shoulder. Mitch looked like he was about to say something. His dad raised his hand and pointed to the scoreboard.

Mitch nodded.

Paige watched for only a moment before looking

down at Emily, who was trying to pull the lanyard off her neck. She let her have it.

Paige took Emily to find water. Jake didn't leave right away. He could see Roberts speaking with the trainers while Mitch had made his way into the cluster of green jackets near the equipment tent.

Jake sat at the bottom step of the bleachers and looked at the oval.

He was still sitting there when he heard footsteps on the track surface. The gritty scuff of a spike dragging against the track. Mitch reached the bleachers and slumped down, the sound of his heavy breathing finally catching up to the noise of his footsteps.

He had a towel around his neck. They looked at the same stretch of track, and neither of them said anything.

"You ran it clean," Mitch finally said.

Jake nodded.

"I mean it." Mitch turned. "The last four hundred. I felt you before I heard you."

"I know," Jake said. "I felt it too."

Mitch exhaled through his nose.

"It's better," he said. "When someone makes you work for it."

Jake looked at him. Mitch was still watching the track, jaw set.

"Yeah," Jake said.

Mitch stood, tossed the towel over his shoulder.

"Next time," he said, and walked away.

Jake watched him go.

He thought about a phone call he couldn't make. His grandmother had died that spring of sophomore year.

The last time he had been at her house she had made him coffee and asked about Paige and Emily in the same tone she used for everything, steady and warm and without judgement.

He would have called her today.

He looked up at the sky and smiled.

Marc Cianfarani

Chapter Thirteen

KidZilla Galaxy on a Saturday afternoon is exactly what it sounds like.

Emily had been talking about it since Monday. Jake wasn't entirely sure how she'd learned the word, but she'd spent three days turning the word 'Galaxy' into a chant. By Thursday, Paige had stopped pretending there was another option.

The noise hit them at the door. Machines, music, the shriek of children. Emily's eyes went wide, and then she was gone pulling toward the nearest flashing light before Jake had his coat off.

They found a table in the corner. Paige slid into the booth and looked around and noticed the far table was having a birthday party and had big Elmo cake on a display table.

"This is fine," she said.

"This is great," Jake said.

She looked at him.

"For her," he added.

Jake took Emily to the ball pit at first. She stood at the edge, suspicious of the scale of it, then stepped in and immediately threw a ball at a child she had never met. The child threw one back. Emily looked at Jake like this was the greatest discovery of her life.

He left her to it.

Back at the table, the pizza had arrived. He ate two slices. Paige ate one and watched the room.

Emily reappeared, cheeks flushed, listing slightly to

the left, pointing back toward the slide.

"Daddy" she said.

He followed her to the slide. She stood at the top gripping the sides, looking down with the focused expression of someone conducting a risk assessment. Then she pushed off and came shooting out at the bottom with a look of pure shock that collapsed instantly into delight.

She was already turning back toward the ladder.

"Again," she said.

They went four more times.

On the fifth, Jake sat her down at the bottom and felt his phone buzz in his pocket. He checked it without thinking. An unknown number. A formal address, a date, time.

Dinner Friday. We'd love to have you both.

Great race! Tom.

He read it twice. It was from Mitch's dad, Tom.

Emily tugged his sleeve toward the ladder.

"One second, Em."

He walked back to the table and handed Paige the phone. She read it once, handed it back, and watched Emily shoot out of the side alone and land in the ball pit with a shriek of triumph.

"We should go," Jake said. "To the dinner."

"I know," Paige said.

She picked up her drink and said nothing.

The machines beeped and flashed. Emily had abandoned the slide and was back in the ball pit, throwing at the same child from before, who had apparently been waiting for her to return.

Jake watched her.

"It's dinner," he said.

Paige closed the message on the phone and slid it into her purse without another word.

The house sat back from the road. Lights glowed through the tall windows. Jake slowed as they walked up the drive, Emily balanced against his chest, Paige beside him.

The green jacket felt heavier than it should.

Paige noticed it before anyone else and smoothed the sleeve, without looking at him. "Looks good on you," she said.

Inside, the air was warm and open. Mitch's mom greeted them first, kneeling immediately to Emily's level, eyes bright.

"Well, hello there," she said. "Aren't you perfect."

Emily stared, then smiled.

Dinner was easy. Stories, laughter, plates passed without ceremony. Mitch's dad asked Jake about training, about patience, about how it felt to finally see things line up.

Paige looked around more than she spoke. The space. The calm. The certainty of it. When she commented on the house, Mitch's mom waved it off.

"Oh, you should see our place in California," she said. "This is what we bought so we could be close while Mitch was here."

"I've never been out of state," Paige said.

"Well," the mom said warmly, "that should change."

After dinner, Mitch's dad rose with his glass. "To Jake," he said. "A hell of a race. Discipline like that doesn't come easy."

Jake looked down at his plate, his thumb tracing the worn edge of his napkin before he spoke.

"If we're toasting anything," he said, lifting his glass, "it should be her."

He pointed to Emily.

"She's the reason I get up early. The reason I come home tired. Everything works because of her."

The table went quiet.

"To Emily," Mitch's mom said.

Glasses clinked.

Later, Mitch's dad gestured toward the back of the house. "Boys," he said. "Come with me."

Jake followed, aware of Paige's eyes on his back as he left the table.

The room beyond was darker, quieter.

The television hummed to life. Belmont Park. The starting gate. A chestnut horse breaking clean into open daylight.

"Watch this," Tom said looking at Jake.

The tape rolled. Secretariat stretched out, smooth, unbothered, the gap behind widening with every stride. Tom spoke.

"From the first step, he decides the race. You don't give anyone comfort. You make them run your race."

Jake watched the screen wide-eyed.

"Once you've got it," Tom said, "don't give it back."

Mitch stood with his arms folded, watching without expression. Jake wasn't sure if Mitch had seen this tape ten times or a hundred.

The blue screen returned.

The room was quiet.

"I used to run like that," Jake said. He didn't mean to say it out loud.

Tom looked at him. "I know," he said. "I've seen the footage."

He clapped Jake on the shoulder on the way out. "You've got the engine," he said. "Don't let anyone tell you to slow down."

Jake found Paige in the hallway.

Emily was asleep against her shoulder with one hand curled loosely under her chin.

Paige looked at his face.

"You look like you remembered something," she said.

Jake almost smiled. "What's that supposed to mean?"

She didn't answer right away. She adjusted Emily's weight on her shoulder, looked down at her, then back at him.

"What did he show you?"

"Secretariat. Belmont Stakes"

She nodded, like the answer confirmed what she'd suspected.

"And?"

"It's about front-running. Controlling the race from the start. Not waiting."

Paige looked toward the hallway where Tom's voice carried from the other room.

"Tom showed Mitch that tape too," she said. "You know that, right?"

She looked at him with the expression she had when

she was deciding how much to say.

"Come on," she said finally. "Emily needs to sleep."

She walked toward the door.

Jake stood there another second in the hallway. Tom's voice behind him, Robert's whiteboard somewhere in the back of his mind.

Chapter Fourteen

The stands were louder than Jake expected. Not roaring, restless.

He jogged a slow loop along the infield, spikes whispering against the track. Coach Roberts stood near the finish line, arms folded, eyes moving, always counting, measuring, somewhere ahead of the race.

Jake rolled his shoulders. He felt good. Too good, maybe. His legs felt twitchy.

He thought of the tape. Decide the race.

They called them to the line. Jake settled into lane two, hands on his hips, breathing steady. Mitch was a few lanes over, loose, unreadable. He didn't look nervous. He never did.

The gun cracked.

Jake broke fast. Instinctively. But instead of easing, instead of letting the surge breathe, he kept pressing. He slid to the front before the curve finished unwinding, felt the lead lock in.

Good, he thought. This was good.

He opened his stride. Let it stretch. Felt taller because of it.

The first lap clicked by clean and controlled. The pack strung out behind him. No one challenged. No one panicked.

On the backstretch the rhythm tightened. His breathing sharpened, but he kept the pace honest, too honest. Every step reached a little farther than it needed to. Every footfall landed ahead of where it wanted to.

At the mile mark, the lactic acid finally caught up. It wasn't a sharp pain, a sudden, thickening in his quads.

He thought of the tape again. Secretariat widening. Never looking back.

He refused to float. Behind him, someone moved. Enough to be felt.

Jake responded the only way the tape taught him how.

He lengthened his stride.

From the infield, Coach Roberts saw it happen. The cadence, the reach.

"Jake! …Jake! Shorten it!" Coach Roberts yelled, now walking quickly towards Jake, "Shorten it!!!"

The voice cut through the noise, sharp and urgent.

Jake heard it.

He reached instead. One more long step, thrown out in front of a tired body, his heel slamming into the track well ahead of his hips. There was a sickening pop, less a sound and more a vibration that traveled straight up his spine.

There was no pain at first. Just shock. Then something was gone. Jake stumbled, instinct kicking in, trying to pretend nothing happened.

One more step, another, and then the pain arrived. Severe and deep.

In the stands, Mitch's mother was standing.

Her hand flew to her mouth. "Oh no," she said, breathless, eyes searching the infield, the fence, the space where Paige should be.

Beside her, Mitch's father didn't rise.

He exhaled. A long, measured breath. The tension

left his shoulders as his gaze shifted, from Jake to the pack surging ahead. To the finish.

Mitch was moving clean now, unchallenged.

The pack flew around him. Mitch slipped past without a word.

Jake stepped off the track and sat hard on the infield grass; hands braced behind him. His heart was still racing like the race never ended.

Coach Roberts was there quickly.

"Don't move," he said, kneeling. His voice was calm, but his jaw was set. "Breathe."

Jake nodded, staring at the curve where the race disappeared.

"I was holding it," Jake said. He wasn't sure who he was talking to. "I didn't want to give it back."

Roberts looked at him.

Marc Cianfarani

Chapter Fifteen

Jake wakes to a ceiling he doesn't recognize, tiles sliding slowly past as someone pushes his bed down a hallway. The pain comes in waves now duller than the track, heavier. Settled.

"Jake."

Coach Roberts' voice reaches him before he can place where he is. He turns his head slightly.

"You're okay," the coach says, "You're stable."

Jake swallows. His throat feels scraped raw.

"Did I finish?" he asks.

Roberts doesn't answer right away. He walks alongside the bed, one hand gripping the rail.

"No," he says. "You did the right thing stopping."

Jake stares back at the ceiling.

"I didn't stop," he says. "My leg did."

They wheel him into a room. Curtains. Beeping machines. Someone slides an IV into his arm. Jake flinches but doesn't say anything.

The door opens again. Paige stands there. Emily pressed against her shoulder. Emily's face is blotchy from crying, eyes wide and confused by the lights and the wires and the unfamiliar quiet.

Jake's chest tightens.

Paige crosses the room in three steps and stops short of the bed, like she isn't sure she's allowed to touch him yet. Her hand hovers, then settles on his forearm.

"You scared me," she says.

"I'm sorry," he says immediately.

She shakes her head. "Don't."

Emily reaches out, fingers grasping for his shirt. Jake lifts his good arm and draws her close, careful of the wires, breathing her in.

"I won," he says. "I was winning."

Paige presses her lips together. She nods once, like she understands exactly what he means.

"I know," she says. "I saw."

A nurse enters, checks his monitors, asks him to rate the pain. Jake gives a number that feels meaningless.

"Doctor will be in soon," she says, turning away.

The door closes.

Coach Roberts clears his throat. "I'm going to step out," he says. "Give you some time."

Jake looks at him.

The coach meets his eyes and nods once.

When he's gone, Paige sits on the edge of the bed.

"What happens now?" she asks.

Jake doesn't answer. He stares at his leg, wrapped and elevated, like it belongs to someone else.

"I need it to heal," he says finally. "I'll be back."

Paige watches him without saying anything.

Emily yawns and rests her head against his chest. Jake hums without thinking, the same low melody he sings when she won't sleep.

The machines keep time around them.

For the first time since the gun went off, Jake lets himself stay still.

He thought about Tuesdays.

Before the injury, Tuesdays were his. Paige covered the early shift, and Jake took Emily to daycare, a small place three blocks from the apartment called Sunridge with a painted mural of animals on the outside wall that Emily had strong opinions about. The elephant was her favorite. She told him this every single Tuesday as they walked past it.

He never had morning practice on Tuesdays. So after drop-off, instead of going straight home, he stayed.

There was a low chain-link fence along the side of the building where the yard opened up, and if you stood at the corner of it you could see the whole play area without being visible from the main entrance. He had discovered this by accident the second Tuesday, when he'd realized he wasn't ready to leave yet and didn't have a reason that made sense in words.

So, he stood at the fence and watched.

Emily moved through the yard with determination. Whatever she was doing, she was entirely inside it. If she was running, she was running with everything she had, arms pumping, hair flying loose from whatever Paige had done to it that morning. If she was standing, still examining the ground, a bug, a pebble, a crack in the concrete that apparently required serious study, the rest of the world ceased to exist for her.

Jake watched her run one morning, reckless and joyful.   He remembered running like that, before it became serious.

He never told her he watched. It was his, this version of her, the one that didn't know she was being seen, and was being herself in a fence yard on a Tuesday morning.

He stayed until the teachers brought the kids inside.

He straightened and walked the two blocks to Maple &
Main.

Maple & Main was a bakery that had been in that
spot longer than the neighborhood deserved. It was
narrow and warm and slightly too loud, and it smelled like
butter and coffee and cinnamon that Jake had never
managed to identify on the menu. He got a coffee. He sat
by the window. He watched the street for forty-five
minutes while the morning sorted itself around him, and
he went and picked up Emily.

This was the part Emily knew about.

When he came through the daycare door, she was
always ready, backpack on, jacket half-zipped, her whole
small body pointed at the exit. She launched herself at him
before he was fully crouched, wrapping her arms around
his neck, and he caught her automatically, like he always
did.

They went to Maple & Main together on the way
home. Always. Without discussion.

Emily always ordered the same thing.

Not approximately the same thing. Not usually the
same thing. The exact same thing. The Blueberry Burst
muffin, which was displayed in the case second from the
left and which Emily approached with the focused energy
of someone completing an important transaction. She
never looked at the other muffins. She never considered
the cookies or the cones or the small paper bags of
croissants that Jake sometimes looked at longingly. The
Blueberry Burst was the muffin, and that was the end of
it.

The woman behind the counter, whose name was

Kayla and who had worked there since before Jake had discovered the place, started setting one out when she saw them come through the door. She never made a production of it. She reached into the case with a square of wax paper and placed it on the counter and gave Emily the look of someone conducting business with a regular.

Emily took this seriously. She always said thank you.

They sat at the small table near the window. The one with the wobbly leg that Jake had learned to compensate without thinking. Emily ate the muffin with deliberate care.

They didn't talk much at the table. This was one of the things he loved most about it. Emily seemed to understand intuitively that some silences weren't empty. She ate her muffin. He drank his coffee. The street moved past the window. The bakery hummed around them.

Sometimes she looked up at him, mid-muffin with a blueberry-stained smile for no reason he could identify, and he smiled back for the same reason.

Lying in the hospital with the machines keeping time around him and Emily's weight settling against his chest, Jake held that Tuesday as carefully as he could. The fence. That yard. Her running without knowing she was being watched. The muffin and the blueberry all over her face.

The doctor uses careful words.

"Complete tear."

The doctor taps the screen, pointing at the gray, frayed ends of the ligament.

"You'll need surgery," the doctor says. "Reconstruction. After that rehab. Months."

Paige sits beside him, Emily asleep in her arms. Paige's free hand rests on Jake's knee careful, protective.

"Full recovery?" Jake asks.

The doctor pauses.

"Our goal is function," he says. "Running is… we'll see how you respond."

Jake doesn't like how that sounds, but he doesn't push. Not yet.

The surgery is early. The room is bright and cold. Jake cracks a joke to the nurse that doesn't land. When the anesthesiologist tells him to count back, he gets to seven.

But before seven.

He stares at the ceiling tiles, counting the seams like he used to count laps. The room smells like nothing. An adjustment near his arm. Someone else moves at the edge of his vision.

He thinks about the race.

Before the fall. The moment he was leading, stride open, the finish line pulling him forward. He was there. He was actually there. He'd spent four years learning how to get to that exact moment and for thirty seconds he had been exactly who he'd always believed he could be.

He wants to stay inside those thirty seconds.

He counts.

Ten. Nine.

He thinks of Emily at the rail.

Eight.

He thinks of the smooth line on Roberts' whiteboard: Timing.

Seven.

When he wakes, his leg feels foreign, heavy, wrapped, distant.

Paige is there. So is Coach Roberts.

And Dolce.

"She insisted," the coach says, bracing for trouble. "Snuck her in my jacket."

Jake almost laughs. It hurts to do even that.

Dolce hops up onto the chair, tail wagging. She rests her chin on the edge of the bed and looks at him.

"Hey," Jake whispers.

Coach Roberts pulls a chair close.

"You did nothing wrong," he says.

Jake looks at him. "I did," Jake says. "I didn't listen."

Roberts shakes his head. "You were competing."

Jake swallows. "What if I can't come back?"

The coach doesn't rush the answer.

"Then you'll still be a father," he says.

Jake looks at Emily. Her chest rises and falls steadily.

"I didn't really have that," Jake says after a moment. "My grandmother raised me."

Roberts listens. Doesn't interrupt.

"I learned to take care of myself early," Jake says. "Guess I never really learned how to stop."

Later, when the afternoon light tilts, Jake thinks he sees Mitch in the doorway. A familiar shape. A pause that feels intentional.

He blinks.

The doorway is empty.

Paige returns after getting coffee.

"Mitch?" Jake asks.

She shakes her head. "No."

The first weeks of recovery are rules.

Jake breaks them all in small ways. He carries Emily when Paige isn't looking. He shifts his weight too soon. He tells himself pain is progress.

It isn't.

The swelling lingers. The strength doesn't come back like the charts say it should. Each week plateaus sooner. At physical therapy, they talk about expectations.

"You're doing well," the therapist says.

Jake hears: This is it.

He argues with doctors. He pushes for timelines. He asks about experimental treatments.

"Your knee may never tolerate impact like it used to," one specialist says, kindly. Final.

Jake leaves furious.

At home, the frustration leaks. He snaps at Paige over nothing. He raises his voice when Emily won't settle. Paige steps between them without saying a word.

Chapter Sixteen

Emily had fallen asleep on the couch, one arm tucked beneath her cheek, the other resting on her stuffed dog. The apartment was quiet.

His knee throbbed.

Jake went to the kitchen cabinet where he kept his pills. He fumbled through to the back of the cabinet, his fingers knocking over a box of Emily's crackers before finding the plastic orange cylinder. He didn't shake it; he unscrewed the cap and stared into the empty bottom.

He sank onto the edge of a chair and pressed both hands over his knee, breathing through the pain. He thought he could ride it out. He thought he could stay.

The pain tightened behind the joint.

He checked the clock.

Emily was asleep.

Paige wouldn't be home for hours.

He opened his phone and called the pharmacy.

"Please," he said, voice low. "Is there any way you can deliver today?"

"No drivers available," the woman replied, apologetic but firm. "I'm sorry."

Jake closed his eyes.

Ten minutes. Maybe less. She won't wake up.

He grabbed his jacket and keys and stood at the door with his hand on the handle.

Then looked at Emily again, small and peaceful.

Opened the door quietly.

Pulled it shut behind him.

Five minutes after he left, Emily stirred.

She sat up, blinking at the empty room.

"Daddy?" she called.

Nothing.

She slid off the couch and padded down the hallway, checking the bedroom, the bathroom, the kitchen.

"Daddy?"

Her voice wobbled. She checked the front door. Still locked. "Mommy?" She tried, louder this time, panic rising.

By the time Paige opened the door that afternoon, arms full of work folders and her hair damp from the rain, she heard the sobs before she saw her.

Emily sat on the floor near the couch, her breathing coming in hiccups. Her stuffed dog pinned under her chin.

"Oh my God," Paige whispered, dropping everything.

"Emily, baby, what happened?"

Emily threw her arms around her, trembling, unable to form the right words.

"Daddy… Daddy …"

Paige's eyes flashed upward, scanning the apartment.

"Jake?" she called, knowing there would be no answer.

Jake returned minutes later, climbing the stairs slowly, clutching a small white pharmacy bag. He froze when he saw their car in the lot. He stopped when he opened the door and saw them. Emily shaking in Paige's arms, Paige pale, furious, terrified.

"What happened?" he asked, voice cracking.

Paige stood. "You left her alone?"

"I thought she was asleep," Jake said. "I thought, I was only going to be gone for a few minutes."

Emily wouldn't look at him.

She buried her face deeper into Paige's neck.

Paige didn't yell. She stood there, her hands still trembling from the adrenaline of the last ten minutes, looking at him like he was a stranger who had broken into their home.

"Why didn't you call me?" asked Paige.

"I couldn't wait."

Jake took a step forward, but Paige stepped back.

Neither of them moved to close the space between them.

Emily still clinging to her, small and shaking.

Paige looked at Jake, at the man she loved and the man who had left their daughter alone in a locked apartment.

Marc Cianfarani

Chapter Seventeen

Emily was on the floor, her tongue poked out in that way she had when she was dead-set on a task. She was beating a plastic cup with a wooden spoon, tap, clack, tap a rhythm that drilled straight into the base of Jake's skull. Paige didn't look up when Jake limped in. She was buried under a drift of hospital bills and "Past Due" notices. She looked tired, dark circles under her eyes.

Jake lowered himself into the chair. His knee didn't scream, it simmered.

"How was physiotherapy?" she asked. Still not looking at him.

"Good," he said. "Fine."

She finally looked up, but not at his face. At his leg. Then she slid a thick, cream-colored envelope across the table. University seal.

"This came today."

He didn't need to open it. It was expected. He'd missed the finals. He'd missed the labs. He looked at the first line: We regret to inform you…

"You said you were at the library," Paige said. "Weeks of that. You said you were finishing your credits so you could graduate in the spring."

"I was there," he said his throat tightening. "I was using the medical journals. Reading up on different procedures that are out there like the LARS procedure. It's an internal brace. Paige. Synthetic. No waiting for a tendon to knit. I could be jogging in six weeks. If I can get to that clinic, the National scouts ..."

"The National scouts aren't coming to this apartment, Jake." She gestured at the peeling laminate, the debt. "And they're not paying the rent. We're three months behind."

"I'm fixing it," he said, sharper than he meant.

"You're chasing ghosts, Jake. You're not here." She stood, chair scraping the floor. "I talked to my mother. She thinks we should stay with her for a while. Until things stabilize."

"For how long?"

"Until you're actually here Jake. Not staring through the walls at a track that isn't there anymore."

She grabbed the diaper bag and began stuffing things in, Emily's lopsided rabbit, a handful of onesies, the scuffed shoes.

She reached for Emily, but the toddler was moving toward Jake. She grabbed his pant leg, tiny fingers locking on.

"Daddy up" she whispered.

He froze. The doctors had been clear. No pivoting. No lifting. No risks.

"Em, honey, let's go," Paige said, her voice shaking. "Daddy's tired".

"Daddy Up!" she insisted, reaching eyes wide and trusting.

"I've got her," he said.

"Jake, don't," Paige warned.

He ignored her. He braced his good leg and scooped Emily up. As he lifted her, the joint buckled. His face went dark. He held her five seconds, maybe less, swaying, quad trembling.

Paige didn't look angry. She looked heartbroken. She saw the sweat on his forehead, his leg shivering under the weight of his own daughter. She stepped in and took Emily from his arms.

"I love you," Paige said, barely a whisper. "But I'm not going to stay here and watch you break yourself into pieces."

The door clicked shut.

When the door closed, the apartment didn't feel empty.

He looked at the wooden spoon.

Chapter Eighteen

Tom pulled into the lot and left the engine running.

The stadium lights were still on. Through the windshield, Mitch could see the auditorium entrance, a few parents arriving late, a trainer holding the door. The banquet started.

His father looked straight ahead.

"Two hours," he said. "The sponsors are driving from Portland. We don't keep them waiting."

Mitch reached for the door.

"You look off," his father said. "What's wrong?"

Mitch watched the building across the lot.

"I was thinking," he said. "Before I go to Texas. Maybe I should stop by and check on…"

"No."

"I didn't finish," Mitch murmured.

"You didn't need to," his father replied. "You don't waste time on distractions. Not now."

"It's not a distraction," Mitch said under his breath.

His father either didn't hear or decided not to.

"Texas is the filter, Mitch. You go down there, you put up the numbers they expect, or you're another kid who had a good college season. We aren't looking in the rearview mirror."

Mitch's jaw tightened.

He got out.

The passenger window rolled down as he walked toward the entrance.

"I'll be back in two hours," his father said. "Don't be late."

The car pulled away before Mitch reached the door.

The auditorium behind the gym never looked more tired than it did during the banquets. The lighting was always bright for the hour. The folding chairs complained every time someone shifted their weight, and the walls, once white, had faded into a shade that looked like old notebook paper. Someone had dragged in a podium from the administration building, the kind with chips across the front where countless rings had knocked into it.

But the banner behind it, that bright blue sheet with the bold black letters, had life in it.

2010 NATIONAL CHAMPIONS

The team filled the seats with restless energy, half dressed in team jacket, half in button-ups that still smelled vaguely of laundry detergent. Their hair was damp from their last practice of the season; their faces still held the glow of youth.

Coach Roberts stood off to the side, watching them talk and tease and laugh. Finally, he stepped toward the podium.

"All right," he said, tapping the microphone even though it didn't need tapping. "Let's settle down."

The voices tapered off.

He looked out at them, rows of young men and women who had spent a year, some four, pushing themselves past what they thought they could be. He took a breath.

"I won't make this long," he said. "You know what this year was. It was 6:00am repeats in the freezing mist when the track felt like a sheet of iron. It was the taste of copper in your throat at the 300m mark. You didn't win because of belief. You won because you didn't quit when your lungs told you to. Some of you thought you didn't have another repeat in you."

A ripple of soft laughter moved across the room.

"But you did it anyway," Coach continued. "That's why you repeated. It wasn't because of luck or talent but because of who you are when no one's looking."

He paused, his voice quieting.

"I'm proud of you. All of you."

Warm applause filled the room.

He shifted his gaze to the seniors.

"To the seniors," Coach said, "the bond you built these four years, that's yours forever. For most of you, that singlet is going into a box tonight. It's going to stay in the back of a closet. But how you ran it. How you bled for it on Monday mornings in the rain, that doesn't wash off. That's yours to keep."

Some of the seniors straightened. Others looked down.

"And for those of you still running," he added, smiling, "I'm a phone call away. Always."

Another wave of applause.

After the speech, the room dissolved into the usual chaos, group photos under the crooked banner, awkward hugs, trainers ribbing each other, parents trying to get one more picture. The team manager attempted a clean team shot, failed twice, and gave up with a laugh.

Coach watched it all from the edge of the room.

The crowd thinned. Jacket zipped. Chairs folded.

Leftover food was boxed and carried out.

Mitch moved through it, said the right things to the right people, shook hands, accepted congratulations with a clean smile. He was good at this part. He had always been good at this part.

He was kneeling beside a chair, folding his warm-up jacket into his duffel, when he glanced toward the doorway.

A few families were still gathered in the hallway. Arms around shoulders. Quick flashes from phones. A father pulling his son into a hug that lasted longer than either of them planned.

Mitch looked away.

He stood and zipped the bag.

Near the exit, a voice caught him.

"Hey. Mitch."

He turned. Shawn was crossing the room with his jacket half on, his father beside him, a man who had been at nearly every home meet Mitch could remember.

Mitch crossed the distance and shook Shawn's hand. "We'll see you, Shawn."

Shawn grinned. "Hey, you remember my dad?"

"Mr.Park," Mitch nodded. "Of course."

"Congratulations on nationals." Mr.Park's grip was firm and warm. "Your parents must be so proud."

"Yeah," Mitch said. "They are."

Mr.Park glanced toward the empty auditorium. "I didn't see them tonight."

"Oh… Yeah. They're back in California."

He held the smile until the door swung shut behind them.

When the noise finally faded, Coach Roberts realized only one runner remained.

Mitch was standing near the back wall, bag over his shoulder looking at the banner.

Roberts crossed the room slowly.

"Camp starts in Texas, soon, doesn't it?"

"Yeah." Mitch shifted the strap on his shoulder. "Armstrong wants us down there in a couple of weeks."

"Keith's good people," Coach said. "He'll take care of you."

"That's what I heard."

"You earned it."

Mitch shrugged. "I guess so."

"You guess so?" Coach asked.

Mitch hesitated. "… feels weird."

"How so?"

Mitch didn't answer right away. His eyes drifted once more toward the doorway, the corridor now empty and dark, the families gone.

"Nothing," he said.

Coach didn't push.

"How's he doing?" Mitch asked.

Coach exhaled.

"I don't know. I've left messages. Only updates I get are from Paige."

Mitch's eyes lifted.

"And?"

"And he's …having a hard time," Coach said. "A really hard time."

Mitch nodded.

Coach stepped forward, offering his hand.

"You take care of yourself."

Mitch shook it. Firm. Respectful.

"You too, Coach."

He headed for the exit.

The door swung open, letting in a rush of cool night air and faint laughter from outside. For a fraction of a second he paused, like a different version of him was considering turning back, saying more, naming what sat unspoken.

But he didn't.

He stepped out into the dark and let the door close behind him.

His father had been to every race that mattered. He had the splits memorized, the film, the strategy sessions that ran past midnight. He had given Mitch every possible advantage.

He just never stayed for the part that came after.

Coach remained in the dim auditorium. The crooked banner sagged slightly behind him. He reached up, straightened it, and let his hand fall.

He turned off the lights.

He closed the door behind him, and the room sank into darkness.

Outside, the night air was cool enough to lift the hair on Mitch's arms.

Chapter Nineteen

Jake pulls the apartment door shut behind him, not entirely sure where he's going. Jacket on, keys in hand, but no plan. The hallway smells faintly of floor cleaner and someone's burnt toast.

But before he takes a step, a door down the hall swings open.

"Jake!"

Ms. Citino's voice is warm as always, like she's greeting a nephew she hasn't seen in a while. Everyone in the building knew her. Always smiling and bubbly.

Her makeup and short black hair set the same way every morning. She's holding a Tupperware and a thermos.

"How did Emily like the muffins?" she asks, smiling with her whole face.

"She loved them," Jake says. "Thank you."

"Oh, that girl," Ms. Citino says, shaking her head fondly. "She's got a sweet tooth like my Tony used to. Could eat a whole tray if you let them."

"How are you doing this morning Ms. Citino?"

"Amazing. Played Bingo last night with some of the girls and you're looking at the big winner!"

"Congrats," replied Jake. "Are you off to work this

morning?"

She waves a hand. "One more year 'til I hit thirty years of service. Can you imagine? Thirty years." She taps her temple.

"That's a long time," Jake says.

"Too long," she says with a little laugh.

She slips her purse over her shoulder, then pauses, her eyes drifting to his apartment door.

"Pretty quiet in there today," she says. "Em still sleeping?"

Jake's throat tightens.

"No. They... they went to visit her mom. Paige wanted a few days with her."

"Oh," Ms. Citino says softly. "That's nice."

"Yeah," Jake clears his throat. "I figured I could use the time alone to …get things sorted. I'm done with school for now, so I'm starting a job search. Trying to find the right fit."

She smiles, reading more than he says.

"You're a determined young man," she says. "You will make it happen."

"Thanks."

She starts down the hall. Jake follows a few steps behind.

But she stops.

Turns.

Her eyes brighten.

"You know," she says, "they're hiring at work."

Jake blinks. "Really?"

"Mmhmm. It's not the job you're looking for, probably. But maybe for now."

She studies him, the tiredness, the lost look.

"If you're not doing anything today, why don't you come with me? Come see. No pressure."

Jake hesitates, "I don't have the car today. Paige took it."

"I bus to work," she says, "I have for years. You can bus for one day."

"I don't know," he says. "I mean, I might need to…"

"Jake"

Her voice softens, but her eyes stay steady.

"Come for today. If you don't like it, you don't come back."

He looks past her towards the exit.

She tilts her head.

"Are you doing anything today?"

He exhales. "No. Not really."

"Good," she says, smiling. "Come on, then. I'll show you around."

She turns and walks. Jake follows.

They step into the cool morning air. Ms. Citino tucks her chin into her scarf, clutching her purse close. Jake shoves his hands into his pockets. They stand at the bus stop, the cold breeze weaving through the street.

The bus arrives with a hiss.

Jake steps on after her.

They sit, she by the window, he in the aisle.

The factory floor hummed through the soles of Jake's shoes, straight up into his bad knee. Jake doesn't mention his knee during the interview. He doesn't mention track at all. He keeps his answers short and steady. When the supervisor asks if he can lift fifty pounds, Jake says yes without hesitation.

The supervisor tells him. "Start Monday."

Jake walks out gripping the paper.

The work is brutal. Standing too long makes his knee swell. Bending sends a hot pulse up his leg. He learns how to shift weight without anyone noticing, how to grit through the sharp parts and live inside the dull ones.

He takes pain killers before and after every shift.

At night, he searches.

Clinical trials. Experimental procedures. Regenerative therapies. Articles filled with promise and disclaimers buried at the bottom. He reads testimonials that sound too good to be true and tells himself that's bitterness talking.

There are places that don't take insurance. Places that talk about healing instead of management.

He saves links. Writes numbers down.

When Paige calls, he tells her about the job. About the progress. He doesn't tell her about the limp getting worse.

"Keep going," she says. "Emily asks about you every day."

He hangs up and goes back to the screen.

He learns how to favor the knee without thinking, how to sleep on his side so the ache doesn't wake him. On paydays, he transfers most of the check into a separate account, labels it treatment.

One afternoon, Paige texts.

Someone reached out.

He waits.

Who? he types.

One of Mitch's parents. His mom.

What about? he asks.

Offering help. She said I don't have to do this alone.

Jake exhales.

That's good, he replies.

Paige sends a heart. He stares at it, then locks the phone and goes back to work.

He keeps searching. One in particular sounds different.

Jake wires the deposit.

That night, he calls Paige.

"I found something," he says. "It could really work. I need a little time."

Paige is quiet, then careful. "I want to believe that."

"I know," he says. "But this is different."

"Okay," she says finally.

After the call, he sits on the edge of the bed, knee throbbing.

Marc Cianfarani

Chapter Twenty

Paige moved through the kitchen, cleaning plates. She didn't rush. She stacked two plates, wiped a crumb from the counter with the edge of her palm, folded a napkin into a neat square.

Her mother was no longer able to help. Her aunt had fallen ill, and her mom had gone to be with her.

She was alone with it again and she understood, in the way you understand things you have understood before and hoped to understand again, that alone was not a temporary condition right now. It was the condition. She had been building around for months, filling the space with routine and Emily's schedule and Mrs. Hughes' visits and the particular reason the building had stopped and she was simply standing in it.

Paige's eyes drifted to the living room.

Emily was asleep on the couch, curled into a little half-moon of blankets. One of her arms dangled off the cushion, her fingers wrapped tightly.

She looked at her daughter and felt the familiar doubling, the love that was so total it had no edges, and underneath it the exhaustion that came from the effort of making sure Emily never saw the exhaustion. That was the invisible labor. The bills or the scheduling or the decisions made alone at kitchen tables. It was the daily performance of a woman who was managing, who was fine, who did not need to be worried about. Emily was five and already too watchful, already too careful with her mother's feelings, and Paige knew this was something she had done, or not prevented, and she carried that knowledge the way you carry something you cannot put down because putting it down would mean admitting how heavy it had become.

The chessboard still sat on the table. Half a game played. Black queen and rook gone. Black king trapped in the corner.

Paige sighed softly and began putting the pieces away, dropping each one into the wooden box with a muted clack.

The headless knight, the bishops, the wooden pawns that rattled against the sides.

She paused at the box, her fingers resting lightly on the rim.

She had watched Emily with these pieces and felt something she couldn't entirely name. Pride, yes, but something more unsettled beneath it. Emily had taken to chess the way she took to everything that offered her a system, a set of rules that held, a world where consequences were logical and traceable and known in advance. Paige understood this about her daughter and understood also where it came from. Emily had learned early that the world did not always behave according to its promises, and so she had developed a preference for the things that did. The chess pieces. The patterns. That certainty of a board where every piece had defined range of motion and could not simply disappear form one square and fail to appear on another.

Mrs. Hughes had given Emily the set. What started as a distraction, a "let's teach her to focus on her mind" gesture, had become a ritual. Emily carried the pieces from room to room like charms. She studied simple tactics from a picture book. She liked the patterns. The certainty.

Paige glanced again at the couch.

Emily still held the white king in her hand, even in sleep.

She finished putting the rest of the pieces away and closed the lid. She walked to the small shelf near the kitchen, the one that held a mismatched row of books and a few framed photos. One photo lay flat, facedown, where she'd placed it the week before.

She told herself she put it face-down because she needed space, which was true as it went. What she hadn't told herself, because some things are easier to do than to explain, was that she put it face-down because she couldn't stop looking at it. She would pass the shelf and her eyes would go there before she'd decided to let them, and she would stand for a moment in the kitchen doorway looking at Jake's face in that photograph, at the quality of his joy in that moment, and she would feel something that had no clean name. It wasn't grief exactly. It wasn't anger. It was something closer to feeling of recognizing a place you once lived in. knowing every room of it and understanding that you no longer have a key.

She picked it up.

It was a picture from the playground back in Springfield. Emily barely walking. Jake kneeling in a ball pit, laughing as she toppled into him. His face was open. Alive. Unguarded.

She looked at it for a long time.

She was trying, as she often did, to locate the moment when that man had become unreachable. It wasn't at the end, that was a different question, that was logistics and failure and the long accumulation of small abandonments before the final one. She meant the earlier moment. The moment when the distance had opened up inside him before it opened up between them. She had seen it happening and had not known how to name it at the time, and now she thought she could name it but naming it was no longer useful. He had decided, somewhere in the long defeat of the injury, that he was only worth knowing as the thing he could do. And when he could no longer do it, he had not been able to find another answer to the question of what he was. She had tried to be the answer. Emily had tried simply by existing. Neither of them had been enough, and she had stopped blaming herself for that approximately six months ago, and some days she almost believed it.

She brushed her thumb across the image.

She placed the photo back on the shelf, face up this time. She wasn't sure why. Some small shift she didn't examine.

She checked her phone.

She walked to the couch. Lifted Emily into her arms. The white king dropped to the floor with a small clatter. Paige picked it up, held it, then placed it inside the wooden chess box.

She carried Emily to bed, laid her down, brushed a strand of hair from her forehead, and closed the door halfway.

In the hallway, Paige let herself breathe.

She stood there longer than she needed to. The apartment was quiet in the way it was quiet after Emily slept, a quietness with texture to it, not empty but held, as though the walls were still paying attention even when she wasn't performing for anyone. She had come to prefer this hour. She had come to need it in a way she hadn't anticipated, the hour when she did not have to be steady for anyone, when she could simply be a woman standing in a hallway with her back against the wall, holding the day at arm's length for just a moment before tomorrow began its approach.

She turned off the lights.

She ended the day.

MORNING

The knock came earlier than she expected. Earlier than she wanted.

Paige rubbed her eyes, padded toward the door in socks, her hair tied loosely from sleep.

She opened the door and froze.

On the landing stood Mrs. Hughes, bright-eyed and warm as ever.

And behind her, to Paige's surprise, stood Mitch.

Paige blinked. Twice.

"Mrs. Hughes …Mitch…hi… this is… wow, this is a surprise."

Mitch's mother stepped forward and hugged her. "We were in the area," she said, then added with a smile, "Well I was in the area. He insisted on driving me."

Mitch offered a small nod. He looked the same but older somehow.

"Hey, Paige," he said.

She responded. "Hey, I didn't know you were back."

"Got in a few days ago," Mitch said. "Got back from England. I'm home for a couple weeks before heading out again."

Paige stepped back to let them in. The apartment filled quickly, familiar in a distant way.

Mrs. Hughes looked around, "So where's my girl? Still asleep?"

Paige gestured toward the hallway. "Exhausted. You got her pretty tired yesterday."

"Oh good," Mrs. Hughes beamed. "Means we did our job."

Paige laughed under her breath. She walked to the counter, picked it up, and held it out.

Emily's white king.

"I also found this in her hand this morning."

Mrs. Hughes burst into laughter. "Oh no! She fell asleep holding it?"

Mitch smirked. "Careful," he said. "Mom's going to try turning her into a grandmaster."

Paige looked at him, genuinely caught off guard, "Wait …you play chess?'

Mitch raised an eyebrow. "Don't look so surprised, Paige."

"But I am."

Mitch leaned against the counter. "In our house, there were two constants: running… and chess."

Mrs. Hughes chimed in, proud: "His father taught him when he was five. He'd solve puzzles before breakfast."

Mitch shot her a look. "Mom."

"What? It's true." She turned to Paige. "Your Emily picks things up the same way. Fast. Focused. It's a gift."

"She loves it," Paige admitted. "Honestly, I think it helps her. Makes her steady."

Mitch nodded, eyes softer than she expected. "It does that."

Then Mrs. Hughes clapped her hands lightly. "Let's see if the sleepyhead is awake. I brought her a new puzzle."

Paige smiled. "She'll love that."

Mrs. Hughes headed down the hallway.

Mitch stayed behind, leaning on the counter, taking in the apartment.

"Hey," he said, "Mom told me things have been hard."

Paige didn't look away. "They've been manageable."

"You're doing a good job," he said.

Paige felt her throat tighten, "Thanks," she whispered.

Mrs. Hughes called out from the hallway, her voice bright. "She's up! And asking if she can be white this time."

Paige laughed, the first real laugh she'd had in days.

Mitch smiled too, small but genuine.

"You two," Paige said, shaking her head. "you've created a monster."

The drive back from Paige's apartment took forty minutes in light traffic.

Tom drove with both hands on the wheel, eyes fixed ahead, the radio off. Mitch had learned young that silence in his father's car usually meant he had made up his mind.

Streetlights moved across the windshield in steady intervals. Storefronts came and went.

His mother had stayed behind to help Paige with Emily. Mitch had driven her there and would have driven her back later. It hadn't seemed complicated. Apparently, it was.

"How often are you going over there?" His father asked.

Mitch kept his eyes on the window. "Over where?"

Tom didn't look at him. "Don't do that."

Mitch waited. "Only a few times. If Mom asks."

His father exhaled through his nose.

"You're in the most important training block of your life," he said. "You know that."

"I'm aware."

"Then start acting like it."

The car stopped at a red light. Neither of them moved.

Mitch looked out at the intersection, at a man in a dark jacket crossing against the signal, at a woman tugging a child along by the hand. When the light changed. Tom drove on.

"This is how people lose their edge," he said. "Not all at once. A little at a time. One wasted evening. One distraction you tell yourself doesn't matter. Then another."

Mitch turned his head slightly. "Driving Mom somewhere isn't going to ruin my season."

"It's not the driving."

Tom adjusted his grip on the wheel.

"Your mother gets attached," he said. "She sees

someone who needs help and makes room for them. Fine. That's who she is. But you don't need to get pulled into every situation she decides to care about."

Mitch felt his jaw set.

"Paige and Emily aren't a situation."

His father's eyes stayed on the road. "You know what I mean."

"No," Mitch said. "I don't."

That got a glance.

"You are twenty four years old," Tom said, "with a real shot at the trials, and right now your life should be very simple. Train. Recover. Compete. That's it. Not somebody else's apartment. Not somebody else's kid."

Mitch turned fully now.

"She's a good kid," he said.

"I'm sure she is."

"And Paige."

Tom cut across him. "Paige is a young woman in a difficult situation. Your mother wants to help. That's understandable. But you need to have better judgement."

The inside of the car went tight and airless.

"Better judgement about what."

His father was quiet, as if deciding how plain he wanted to be.

"About where you spend your time," he said. "And who you spend it with."

Mitch looked at him.

"Say it."

Tom kept his voice level. That was always his way. He almost never sounded cruel when he was being cruel. He sounded certain.

"You could have anyone," he said. "And instead you're hanging around a girl with a kid and a whole mess attached to her. That is not your problem, Mitch. Don't make it your life."

Mitch went still.

He looked back out the window, then forward again.

"Pull over," he said.

His father gave a short, disbelieving breath. "Don't be dramatic."

"Pull over."

Mitch thought he might refuse.

Then Tom put on the signal, eased to the curb, and stopped. The hazard lights started clicking, orange against the dark.

Neither of them spoke.

Cars passed. A siren moved somewhere far off then farther.

Mitch looked at his father.

"Don't talk about them like that," he said.

Tom's face didn't change. "I'm telling you the truth."

"No," Mitch said. "You're saying what you think you can get away with saying."

His father turned forward with him then, more irritated than angry.

"You're losing perspective."

Mitch reached for the handle.

"You don't get to talk about my mother like she's foolish," he said. "And you don't get to talk about Paige and Emily like that either."

Tom's mouth tightened.

"This is exactly what I mean," he said. "Emotion

over judgement."

Mitch opened the door. Cold air rushed in.

"Mitch."

He paused, one foot on the pavement.

"If you walk away from this," Tom said, "you are proving my point."

Mitch stood there, hand still on the door.

He looked back.

"No," he said. "I'm hearing you clearly."

For the first time, his father had nothing to say.

He sat there behind the wheel, hazard lights washing his face orange.

Mitch stepped out, closed the door.

He stood on the sidewalk without fully meaning to. Waiting for his father to get out. Or roll down the window.

The car pulled away from the curb and merged back into traffic, without another word.

Mitch watched the taillights until they disappeared.

He turned and started walking.

The cold hit harder once he got moving. He shoved his hands into his pockets and kept a steady pace, his breath settling after the first few blocks.

At the first main intersection he took out his phone.

His Mother's name sat near the top of his recent calls.

He looked at it, then put the phone back in his pocket.

She was with Paige and Emily. Let her stay there.

He crossed on the light and kept going. He walked the rest of the way home.

Marc Cianfarani

Chapter Twenty-One

The call comes in the middle of a shift.

Jake is stacking pallets when his phone vibrates in his pocket. He ignores it at first. It vibrates again. He steps aside, wipes his hands on his jeans, answers without looking at the screen.

"Jake," the voice says.

It's one of the assistant coaches.

"I'm sorry," he continues. "It's Coach Roberts. He passed early this morning."

Jake leans back against the wall. The concrete is cool through his shirt.

He puts the phone on speaker, and the assistant coach's voice continues, but the forklift drowns him out.

"They think it was his heart," he says. "He went quick."

Jake's other hand opens the browser. The clinic page loads. He scrolls while the coach talks.

The man hesitates. "There'll be a service this weekend. I wanted to make sure you knew."

"Thanks for calling," Jake says.

The call ends and the page stays open. He stays where he is with the phone still in his hand. The machines keep running. Someone shouts for a forklift. Nothing slows down.

On break, he sits alone on an overturned crate staring at his leg. He asks the manager if there is any overtime available.

That night, Paige calls.

"Are you okay?" she asks, before he can say hello.

"Yeah," Jake says. "Tired."

She hesitates. She has learned to read his tiredness the way you learn to read weather in a place you have lived a long time. There is the tiredness that is physical, the factory shifts, the knee, the hour. And there is the other tiredness, the one that sits behind his eyes and has nothing to do with sleep, the one that had been there since before the injury and simply found the injury to lie inside. She could hear which one this was.

"I heard about Coach Roberts."

"Oh," Jake says again. "Yeah. He passed."

Her breath catches.

"Jake… I'm so sorry."

"Thanks."

Paige is waiting….

"Are you going to the service?" she asks.

"I don't think so."

"Why not?"

He looks at his knee, swollen slightly, skin tight. "I've got work," he says. It sounds reasonable.

Another pause. Longer this time.

"Jake," she says, "this was someone who mattered to you."

"I know."

"But you're acting like ..."

She stops.

"What is that?"

Jake blinks. "What?"

"That noise. There's a noise."

He looks at the ceiling. The window. Somewhere outside a car idling.

"Nothing," he says. "Probably outside."

"Jake." Her voice sharpens. "that's not outside. That's ...Jake, do you have the stove on?"

He doesn't answer immediately.

The sound arrives then. Not new ... suddenly audible. A high whistling that has apparently been going on long enough to fill the apartment without him noticing.

"Jake. Jake. Is something on the stove?"

He stands. Crosses the kitchen in three steps. The kettle wasn't whistling; it was piercing. He must have put in on forty minutes prior. He lifts it off the burner and the whistling dies.

"Sorry," he says, "Kettle."

Paige is quiet.

"You didn't hear it," she says.

"I heard it," he says.

She doesn't argue. There is no version of this argument that ends anywhere good. She knows what she heard, which is a man who did not hear a kettle screaming because he was not inhabiting his own apartment, and he knows what he needs her to believe, which is that everything is being managed, and she has learned that some nights the most useful thing she can do is let him believe she believes it.

She did not believe it.

"I'm handling it," he says finally.

Paige exhales. "That's what scares me."

After the call Jake opens his laptop. The clinic's page loads quickly now, saved to his favorites. There's an email waiting, confirmation, next steps, instructions.

The service happens without him. People speak about Coach Roberts' integrity. They remember the way he cared for his runners like family.

That night, Paige texts. "I wish you'd gone."

Later, lying awake, Jake stares at the ceiling. He thinks of the coach's voice…shorten it… and realizes he can't remember the sound of it anymore.

Chapter Twenty-Two

The office door had been left open.

Nobody could agree on who did it. Later, each of the assistant coaches would gesture at someone else with the conviction of people who were certain it wasn't them. The trainer said it was the equipment manager. The equipment manager said it was the trainer. The graduate assistant, who had only been there six weeks and was still learning everyone's name, said nothing and looked at the floor.

None of it mattered.

Because Dolce was gone.

She hadn't bolted exactly. She had noticed the open door, assessed the situation with the calm intelligence of an animal who had been around athletic facilities long enough to know that chaos and opportunity often arrived together, and walked out at a measured, dignified pace.

By the time anyone noticed, she was on the track.

Coach Hendricks saw her first from the infield. He stopped mid-sentence, squinted, and said, "Is that…"

"Yeah," said the trainer beside him.

They looked at each other.

"Okay," Hendricks said. "Okay. Let's ... walk toward her. Calmly. Don't make it a thing."

They walked toward her calmly.

Dolce watched them approach with what could only be described as mild interest. She waited until they were perhaps four meters away, close enough that Hendricks was reaching out a hand, and then she was elsewhere. Not a sprint. More of a suggestion of movement. She had reallocated herself twenty meters down the backstretch in seconds.

"Don't run after her," Hendricks said immediately.

The graduate assistant, who started running, stopped.

"It excites them," Hendricks said. "If you run, they think it's a game."

A short silence.

"Is it not a game?" the trainer asked.

Hendricks watched Dolce execute a leisurely loop around the far curve. "I think it might be a game."

Word spread fast around the track facility, and it picked up embellishment as it went. Within ten minutes there were seven people on the infield, all of them trying different strategies.

Coach Ferrell crouched low and made soft encouraging sounds.

Dolce watched him from a distance of fifteen meters, decided this was not a posture she needed to engage with, and trotted briskly in the other direction.

The equipment manager tried circling wide to cut her off. Dolce waited, let him complete his arc, and then slipped through the gap he'd left behind him with an ease that suggested she had mapped the entire operation before he had taken his first step.

"She's doing it on purpose," someone said.

"She's a dog," Hendricks said.

Dolce sat down at the top of the curve and appeared to yawn.

Mitch was crossing the parking lot with his duffel when he heard the noise. He stopped. Looked through the gate. Processed what he was seeing. Walked in.

"What's happening," he said.

"The dog got out," Ferrell said, slightly out of breath.

Mitch looked at Dolce, who was now doing a slow circuit of the infield with the unhurried energy of someone on a Sunday stroll.

"I'll get her," he said.

Several people started to speak at once. Mitch had dropped his bag. He stretched his quads briefly, shook out his arms, and settled into his stance with the focus of a man who had run conference finals and national heats and did not intend to be defeated by a medium-sized dog in front of his former teammates.

He launched and he was gaining. His stride opened up like it always did when the race demanded it, clean and powerful, the gap closing.

Dolce glanced back. Once.

The look lasted perhaps half a second. Then she shifted through a gear that, by accounts, should not have existed, and the gap did not close again.

Mitch ran the full back stretch at close to his race pace. Dolce stayed ahead of him by precisely enough to make it clear the margin was her choice. When he surged, she extended it by three meters. When he eased, she pulled it back to two.

At the far curve Mitch finally stopped, hands on knees, chest heaving. Dolce slowed to a trot, circled back to a point approximately ten meters away, and sat down to watch him recover.

The infield was completely silent. Then someone started laughing. Then Ferrell, who had not meant to, pressed his hand over his mouth and failed entirely to stop it.

Mitch straightened up, still breathing hard, and looked at the dog. Dolce looked back at him with the expression of an animal that had made its point and was now waiting to see what came next.

"Roberts," Mitch said to no one in particular, still catching his breath, "would have absolutely loved this."

Nobody argued with that.

They tried everything.

Ferrell's encouraging crouch. A length of rope that Dolce treated as an interesting obstacle rather than a threat. Someone suggested calling her name in a firm authoritative voice, which achieved nothing except making the graduate assistant feel briefly useful.

Dolce moved at her own pace around the track, occasionally sitting, occasionally trotting, occasionally breaking into those brief full-speed bursts that made everyone freeze and then exhale when she curved back rather than heading for the open gate.

She wasn't going anywhere. She was not coming in.

It was Mitch who spotted him first.

A man making his way down from the stands with

the careful deliberate momentum of someone who had committed to a course of action and was not entirely sure it was a good idea. He was broad-shouldered, carrying a few extra decades around the middle, wearing a polo shirt that had seen better days and the expression of a man who had been sent on an errand by his wife and taken a wrong turn somewhere. He was holding a large paper bag from the sandwich place two blocks over.

He stopped at the edge of the track, looked at the assembled coaches, looked at the dog, and looked back at the coaches.

"Is this the track team?" he asked.

"Yes," said Hendricks.

The man said. "My kid has practice at four. I brought lunch." He held up the bag. "I might have the wrong facility."

"You do," said Hendricks. "Middle school is on Brennan Street."

"Right," the man said. He didn't leave immediately. He looked a Dolce again. "That your dog?"

"It's complicated," said the trainer.

The man reached into the bag, like you do when you're standing somewhere awkward and need something to do with your hands, and produced a large soft pretzel. He looked at it, Looked at the dog.

"Does she like …."

"Don't" said Farell.

The man's hand was in the air.

"TREATS," he announced, with the full enthusiasm of a man who had raised a Labrador for eleven years and knew exactly how this worked.

What happened next was, by all witness accounts, instantaneous.

Dolce, who had spent the better part of an hour evading seven reasonably athletic people with practiced, almost artistic ease, turned toward the sound. Her ears went up. Her whole body reoriented. And then she ran. Not the teasing, controlled canter of the last hour. The real thing.

Full extension, full commitment, the white and brindle blur that had reduced Mitch to a bent-over gasping wreck now pointed at a pretzel in an outstretched hand and operated at an entirely different velocity.

She covered the distance in the time it took most of the assembled coaches to process what was happening.

The man barely had time to brace.

Dolce planted both front feet on his considerable midsection, snatched the pretzel from his hand with surgical precision, dropped back to all fours, and began eating with the calm satisfaction of someone who had always known exactly how the afternoon was going to end.

The man looked down at her.

Then up at the coaches.

"You're welcome," he said.

Later, after Dolce had been leashed and the man had been given directions to Brennan Street and Mitch had collected his bag from where he'd dropped it, the infield went quiet again, as it had been quiet all week.

Ferrell stood near the start line and looked at the empty track.

Hendricks came and stood beside him.

Neither of them said anything.

"He really would have loved that," Ferrell said finally.

"Yeah," Hendricks said.

Chapter Twenty-Three

The clinic's website looks clean.

Smiling faces. Words like healing and return. Jake scrolls past testimonials that read like victory laps, former athletes, before-and-after photos, timelines that promise neat endings.

The man on the phone speaks calmly, confidently. He never interrupts. He uses Jake's name often, like a reassurance. He explains the treatment, stem cells, and regeneration. Tells him it's a process, not a gamble.

"It's not covered by insurance," the man says. "But that's usually the case with real innovation."

Jake nods, even though the man can't see him.

"How long until improvement?" Jake asks.

"A few months," the man says. "Some patients feel changes sooner."

Jake wires the money in pieces. Savings first. Then the envelope he's been pretending isn't emergency-only anymore. That night, scrolling through old emails, he notices a missed voicemail he's never played.

Coach Roberts.

He presses the phone to his ear. "Hey, kid. Checking in… I know it's rough right now, but listen, don't shut down on me. You hear? You don't have to carry this alone. Call when you're ready."

His thumb hovers over the button to replay it. He doesn't. He deletes it instead. And instantly regrets it.

When Paige calls, he tells her about the treatment.

"Mexico?" she asks.

"It's legitimate," he says quickly. "I did the research. This is different."

In the background he can hear the quiet of after Emily's bedtime. Dishes being stacked. A chair scraping once against the floor.

"If it works," she says, "that would be… incredible."

"I'll get back," he says. "I'll fix this."

"I know you want to."

Not I want that but I know you want to,

Jake heard the difference and said nothing.

"How's Emily?" he asks.

"She's good." She adds. "She keeps your shoes by the door. The old ones. I haven't moved them."

"Tell her I called," he says.

"She knows you called. She asks every morning."

"I'll fix this, Paige."

"Okay," she says.

He sits with the word after she hung up. Turns it over. Tries to find the belief inside it. He opens the laptop instead.

His knee feels warm and heavy under the bandage when he shifts on the hotel bed that evening. The doctor warned him that might happen.

He calls Paige from the hotel room, sitting on the edge of the bed with the curtains open.

She picks up on the second ring because she always picked up on the second ring when it was Jake. The first ring she used to compose herself. The second she answered before she could decide not to.

Emily was asleep.

Paige stood at the kitchen counter with the phone against her ear and the laptop open beside her, the browser tab she hadn't closed still sitting there in the background. She'd found it four days ago.

A running forum with forty-three replies under a thread titled Mexico Sports Recovery Clinic. Anyone Tried This? She'd read all forty-three. She'd read them twice. Then she'd called Jake and told him carefully, starting with concern instead of conclusion.

He listened.

"You can find anything online," he said. "People complain about everything."

She hadn't pushed. She'd made a note of not pushing. Because she knew what pushing would sound like to him, and it wasn't I'm worried about the money or I'm worried about us. What it would sound like was your career is over and we both know it and she wasn't willing to say that. She wasn't sure she believed it. She only knew the forum thread had thirty-one posts using the word scam and that Jake had closed the laptop himself and changed the subject to Emily's new thing with chess, and she let him.

"Hey," she said. "How did it go?"

"Good," he said. "Real good."

He put a slight extra weight on real. It was the first thing she noticed. Jake had always been a bad liar to people who knew his voice. The confidence was there but needed to be held up. She recognized it from before races. The difference was that before races it had been real underneath.

She moved the laptop slightly without looking at it.

"The doctor was thorough," Jake said. "More thorough than anyone back home. He looked at everything, the original scans, the surgery notes, all of it. He said the approach they use here addresses the nerve pathways, not just the structural damage. That's why standard treatment hasn't worked. It's not the tissue, it's the signal."

She knew those words. It wasn't because she'd heard them from Jake before, but because she'd seen their shape in the clinic's website. She'd spent an evening on that website two weeks ago while Emily slept, reading and rereading the language. Nerve pathway restoration. Addressing root cause rather than surface damage.

She had not told Jake she'd gone back to the website.

"That sounds promising" she said.

She was careful. The word she always chose when she needed to say something that wasn't a lie but wasn't the full truth either.

"It is. It's more than promising, Paige. These are people who have actually fixed this. Not manage it. Fixed it."

She waited. Somewhere behind her the refrigerator made its low cycling hum. In the hallway the nightlight threw its small circle of yellow onto the floor outside Emily's door. Paige looked at it.

She thought about Emily asking that morning whether Daddy was coming home soon. She had answered the way she always answered, careful and true as far as it went, I don't know when baby, but he's working on things, and Emily had nodded, which meant she had understood more than Paige had said and had decided not to press it.

"How much was it?" Paige asked.

"We talked about that."

I know. I just. She stopped. There was no version of the end of that sentence that didn't sound like accusation. The words lined up in her head anyway. I needed to know how deep this was. I needed to know what we're working with when this doesn't work. I needed to know how to plan for what comes after, and I can't plan if I don't have numbers.

"I know," she said instead.

In the background she could hear the hotel room around him. She had a sudden and unwelcome image of him sitting on the edge of a bed she'd never seen with a knee he'd paid too much to fix and a receipt in his pocket, and she pressed her lips together and made herself stay in her own kitchen.

The thing she had not said to her mother or to anyone, was that she still wanted it for him. She still wanted it desperately, the recovery, the return, the man who had crouched beside her on a curb in Springfield and said I promise. She wanted that man back with an intensity that embarrassed her when she examined it too closely, because wanting it this much after everything felt like a weakness she should have outgrown.

She had not outgrown it.

"Jake," she said. Her voice shifted without her meaning it to. "I want this to work. I really do."

And she did. That was the thing she needed him to understand and couldn't find the right arrangement of words for. She wanted it not for the running, she had stopped believing in the running a long time ago and she knew he knew this and they had both agreed not to say it. She wanted it because she remembered what Jake was like before the injury, his determination when he was moving toward something and his joy for life, and she missed that person.

"It is," he said.

"Okay"

"Paige."

"I said, okay."

She heard him start the sentence she'd heard him start so many times she could finish it herself. I'm going to fix this. I'm going to come back and I'm going to fix this and everything is going to

"Jake."

She said it softly. Not cutting him off.

"Come home safe."

She stood in the kitchen after the call ended and didn't move. The laptop was still open beside her. The forum tab was still there. Thirty-one replies. She reached over and closed the browser without reading it again. She knew what it said.

She sat down at the kitchen table.

The bills were where she'd left them. The ones that could be paid and the ones that couldn't. She pulled the pile toward her and sorted them. She made two lists on the back of an envelope. One column for what she knew how to handle alone. One column for what she didn't.

The second column was longer. She looked at it and then folded the envelope and put it in the drawer under the takeout menus where she kept things she wasn't ready to look at directly.

She thought about what alone was going to have to mean now.

And the alone was not the temporary kind of alone of a man who was away and coming back. The other kind that required you to stop dividing the problems into yours and his and simply start solving them because there was no his anymore, or there was, but his was somewhere in Mexico in a hotel room that she had never seen, getting injections that thirty-one people on the internet had called a scam, and the rent was due and Emily needed new shoes and the second column was longer than the first.

She folded the envelope and put it in the drawer.

She was not ready.

She was going to have to be anyway.

On the counter her phone lit up.

Mrs. Hughes asking if Emily wanted to come for dinner Saturday. Paige looked at the message.

She typed yes.

She set the phone face down and sat in the quiet kitchen.

She thought about the woman her mother had been when she was Emily's age. The quality of her mother's competence, the way she moved though difficulty without drama, the way she made the absence of a man look like choice rather than a wound. Paige had watched her mother do that her whole childhood and had absorbed it without meaning to, the discipline of it, the refusal to perform helplessness. The quiet insistence on managing.

She had thought for a long time this was strength.

She still thought it was strength.

She also thought, for the first time sitting on this night, that it had a cost that her mother never named. That the woman who never asked for help and never showed the wound and always had the second column handled had also been, in some room Paige had never been allowed into, a woman who was exhausted and frightened and wanted someone to sit with her in the dark without her having to explain why.

Paige sat in the dark.

She did not turn the light back on.

Chapter Twenty-Four

The receptionist doesn't look up immediately.

Jake stands at the desk with his jacket still on, the appointment confirmation folded in his front pocket.

She types. Finishes. Looks up.

"Name?"

He gives it.

She types again. "ID please."

Jake reaches into his back pocket.

Then the inside of his jacket.

He stands very still, hands pressed flat against his sides.

"I don't have it on me," he says.

The receptionist's expression doesn't change. "We require government issued photo ID for all new patients."

"I have the confirmation," Jake says.

He produces the folded paper and sets it on the desk.

"Email confirmation. My name, the date, the time. Everything's there."

She glances at it. "I understand. We still need ID."

"I don't have it today." His voice still even. Barely. "I can bring it next time."

"We'd need to reschedule."

"I can't reschedule."

"The next available appointment with Dr...."

"I can't reschedule." The evenness leaves his voice. "I've been waiting for three months for this. I lost ..." he stops. Starts again. "I need to see him today."

She reaches for the phone with practiced calm of someone who had done this before, who has a procedure for exactly this escalation and intends to follow it.

"Sir, I understand you're frustrated …"

"You don't." The words come out harder than he intends. "You have no idea. I've had surgery. I've had rehab. I flew to Mexico with money I didn't have because someone told me they could fix this and they couldn't fix anything. They took everything I had and I'm still …" his voice cracks on the last word. He presses his mouth shut.

The waiting room goes very quiet.

He is aware of the other chairs. Of their careful avoidance of his eyes.

"Please," he says. Quieter now. The anger burns through whatever is holding it. "Please. I need to see him."

The receptionist holds his gaze. Then she picks up the phone. Turns slightly away. Says something too low for Jake to hear. She listens and then sets the phone down.

"The doctor will see you," she says. "Please take a seat."

Jake stands there a moment longer than necessary.

"Thank you," he says.

She has looked back at her screen.

He finds a chair. Sits. Places his hands on his thighs where they won't shake. He has learned the choreography of waiting. He hasn't needed to relearn it from scratch in a waiting room before. The clinic is quieter than the other. No posters promising recovery. No smiling athletes, frozen mid-stride. Beige walls.

The doctor is old, his skin like crumpled parchment as he scans the chart. He doesn't rush. His thumb hovers over the imaging report, the spot where Jake knows the failed experimental results are buried.

"Surgery, rehab… the works," the doctor says, mostly to the chart.

Jake nods. He is tired of explaining.

The doctor turns the screen. There is the knee. A grainy mess of hardware and bone. "Structurally? You're a success story. The ligament is tight. Stable."

"Then why does it feel like a hot iron is twisting in there every time I take a step?" Jake says. Sharper than he means.

The doctor doesn't react.

"Because your brain is still stuck on the day you tore it," he says. "Like an alarm that never shut off. The damage is gone, but the signal isn't."

Jake leans back, the air leaving his lungs.

"So nothing's actually wrong."

"Your knee may still swell or flare if you overload it," the doctor adds. "It isn't fragile, but it is sensitive. But…it's in your nerves. Physical, but it can't be fixed with a scalpel. You have chronic pain."

Jake looks away.

"You can walk. You can jog," the doctor says. "but racing…"

He exhales, a small, tired sound.

"That's pushing it."

"Will it ever get better?" Jake asks.

"It can," the doctor says. "Often does."

He glances back at the chart.

"I can refer you to a pain specialist," he adds. "They try targeted injections sometimes. For some people they get improvement from it."

A pause.

"Not for everyone."

Jake nods once, though he isn't sure what he is agreeing to.

Outside, the dry Oregon heat needles his skin.

Jake stands on the pavement outside the clinic and doesn't move. The streets are busy with mid-morning traffic. He starts walking. Not toward anything. Walking, because standing still becomes impossible and motion keeps the thoughts from stacking.

He has spent two years, building a case. That is what he understands now. Two years of scans and clinics and wired deposits and phone calls to men with smooth voices who used his name too often. Two years of telling Paige this one is different, of telling himself the knee is the obstacle and the knee is the only thing standing between him and the life that had been interrupted.

The knee is stable. Has been, probably for longer than he wants to calculate. He turns a corner without choosing to. A small park opens up on his left, the kind that exists between buildings.

Two benches. A man eating a sandwich on the far bench, reading on his phone.

Jake sits on the other bench. He presses his palms flat against his thighs, like he used to before races, grounding himself through the hands, and looks at the pavement between his feet.

He has been so certain pain was proof. Proof the

injury was real, proof that everything he has lost has been taken from him was physical and external and not his fault. The pain has been evidence.

He sits with that.

At some point his face is wet. He doesn't notice it starting and he doesn't try to stop it.

He sits on the bench in the small park between buildings and he cries for the first time since the track, since the moment his knee popped.

He cries for Roberts, grief arriving late. He cries until the man with the sandwich finishes eating and leaves, and the bench across from him is empty. Then he wipes his face with the back of his hand. Sits up straight. And for the first time in two years, feels no urge to open his phone and search.

The office smells different without him. No coffee. No peppermint gum.

Coach Hendricks and Coach Ferrell stand in the doorway, silence pressing between them.

"Someone has to take her," Hendricks finally says.

The whippet lies curled under Roberts' old chair, head resting on her paws, eyes open but unfocused.

"Shelter?" Ferrell offers.

"No. He'd kill us."

"She can't stay here."

The trainers are cleaning out the training room nearby, tossing old tape rolls, stacking cones, wiping down clipboards that still have Roberts' handwriting on them. Every sound echoes too loudly.

Then one of the athletic trainers appears in the

doorway. Laura. The younger one, whose sneakers always squeak on the gym floor. She stands there a moment, eyes on the dog, says nothing.

Then. "I'll take her."

Both coaches turn. She holds their stares but her voice softens.

"My daughter's been begging for a dog for months. Made a whole list of reasons why we need one." A small pause. "She cries every night because we keep saying no."

She looks at Dolce. "I think she'd love this one."

Dolce lifts her head slightly, ear twitching at the sound of a new voice.

"You sure?" Hendricks asks.

Laura adds. "She deserves a soft place. And my kid will fuss over her until she doesn't remember anything else."

Coach Ferrell rubs his eyes. "Roberts would've liked that."

Laura crouches beside the dog. Dolce sniffs her hand. Cautious, but gentle.

"Hey sweetheart," Laura whispers. "You ready to come with us?"

Dolce doesn't move. But when Laura strokes her head, she doesn't pull away either.

"Let us know if you need anything," Hendricks says.

"And ... thanks," Ferrell adds.

Laura clips on the leash. Dolce stands slowly, as if unsure whether she still has a pack to follow.

As they walk down the hallway, Dolce pauses once, turning back toward the office, ears perked.

Then she keeps walking.

Chapter Twenty-Five

The buzzer was a needle in the quiet. Ten past nine.

Paige didn't move. She stayed in her robe, hand curled around a mug that had long ago stopped steaming. In the next room, the scrape of Emily's spoon against the ceramic bowl was demanding. Paige pressed the button without asking who it was.

The elevator began its groan.

The thought came again.

Her mother.

The woman herself, she was miles away, likely doing exactly this, sitting in a kitchen at ten past nine with cold coffee and the particular stillness of a woman who had learned to occupy her own silence without flinching. It wasn't about the woman but the shape of it. The cold coffee. The pajamas at mid-morning. The apartment that belonged entirely to her because there was no one else for it to belong to. Paige had watched her mother inhabit that shape her entire childhood and had told herself, with the confidence of someone who had not yet been tested, that she would not become it. That her life would be structured differently. That she had chosen differently.

She had chosen differently.

The choosing had not been enough.

She stood at the counter and tried to shake it off. It stayed. The comparison sitting in her chest with the particular weight of things that are true and unwelcome simultaneously.

She had called her mother at eleven the night she

moved in. She hadn't wanted to, but the silence in the new kitchen had pressed in until she picked up the phone. Her mother had answered instantly, the way she always answered.

Paige talked.

About the boxes, the ceilings. The way Emily wouldn't let go of Jake's old shoes, carrying them from room to room like an artifact from an excavation, something recovered from a life that had existed and stopped existing and needed to be kept anyway. She talked about the quality of the first night's silence, how it was different from the silence she had been living inside for months in the apartment they had shared, how that silence had been dense with Jake's absence, thick with everything unsaid between them, whereas this silence was simply empty, clean and terrible in its emptiness, a silence that didn't mean anything except that she was alone and this was where alone lived now.

Her mother didn't interrupt.

When Paige stopped, there was a pause. Then a sentence. Flat. Final. The kind that could only come from a woman who had lived it and come out the other side and knew exactly which truths were useful and which ones only felt useful.

You cannot want it more than he wants it for himself.

Paige had hung up and sat in the dark. Three weeks later she was still sitting with it. It wasn't because she hadn't understood it. She had understood it immediately, had felt it land with the precision of something that had been true for longer than she had allowed herself to know. She was sitting with it because she had not yet found the passage between them.

"Em, finish."

Emily didn't look at her. She looked at the door. The elevator reached their floor, a metal sigh. Paige opened it before the knock could come.

Mitch stood in the hallway in a grey t-shirt and gym shorts, a large flatpack box balanced on one shoulder, another leaning against the wall.

"Delivery," he said.

Paige looked at the box, then his face. "Mitch."

"I also do assembly," he said. "But that's extra."

Behind her, Emily's chair scraped.

"Eat, Emily."

The chair scraped back.

Mitch moved past her. He brought the first box in, then the second. He didn't ask where they went. He looked at the wall, then the window, and set them down by the light.

They began.

She handed him the brackets. Watched him. He read the instructions once, and dropped them to the floor. He didn't look at them again. He didn't misalign the panels. He didn't stop to reconsider. He moved through the assembly with the focused economy of someone who had decided what he was doing before he arrived and was simply executing the decision.

Jake would have.

The thought arrived before she could prevent it, which was how it always arrived, without announcement, inserting itself into the present moment with the casual authority of something that lived there permanently.

Jake would have read the manual twice. Slowed at the third step. Stopped to reconsider the fourth. He would have laid all the pieces out on the floor first, counting them against the diagram with the methodical thoroughness he brought to everything he didn't fully trust himself to get right, which was most things outside of running. She would have stood beside him with the screwdriver, waiting, and he would have felt her waiting and become slightly more tense because of it, and she would have noticed the tension and tried to make herself less present, and the whole thing would have taken forty minutes and ended with the shelves slightly uneven and both of them pretending not to notice.

She had loved that about him.

She had found it maddening.

Both of those things were true and she was old enough now and tired enough now to stop requiring them to resolve into one.

Under it the other thing arrived too, the thing that always followed the Jake thought, quiet and unwelcome and persistent.

I hope he's okay.

It wasn't a feeling out of an obligation or as the residue of a relationship she was still attached to. But as something genuine and unresolved that she had not been able to excise no matter how much time passed or how much distance grew between the woman she was now and the woman who had sat on a curb in Springfield at eighteen and let herself be promised to.

She handed Mitch a screw. Her fingers were shaking slightly. She pressed them flat against her palm before extending them again.

"Do you run?" Emily asked from the couch.

"Yeah."

"Is that why your legs are like that?"

"Like what?"

"Big."

Mitch looked at his legs, then at her. "Yes," he said. "That's exactly why."

He tapped a panel into place with the heel of his hand. Solid. Final.

"Left of the window was right," Paige said.

"Usually am."

Mitch stood, straightening.

"Are you leaving?" Emily asked.

"Got training."

"You didn't put anything on them yet."

"That's the fun part," Mitch said. "That part's yours."

Paige walked him to the door.

The words gathered somewhere in her throat but didn't come out. She had been assembling them for the last hour, various versions of the same sentence, thank you for this, thank you for showing up, thank you for not requiring an explanation or an accounting of that I need and why. She couldn't find the right version. They all sounded insufficient and they were insufficient. What Mitch had done by arriving this morning with flatpack boxes and no agenda was not a thing she had a proportionate response for because it was not a proportionate gesture. It was simply a person deciding that someone else needed something and providing it without making the providing into an event.

She had not realized how much she had needed that until it was happening.

"Tell your mom thank you."

"Tell her yourself," he said.

He took the stairs.

She stood in the doorway after he left.

She was listening, she realized. For the sound of his steps moving down the stairwell. They were unhurried, regular, the sound of someone leaving without urgency, without the performance of departure. She tracked them down one flight, then the half-landing, then the second flight until they faded into the ambient noise of the building and she could no longer separate them from it.

She stayed there longer than she needed to.

She was aware that she was doing it and she did it anyway.

There was something in this that she needed to look at and she looked at it. The listening for his footsteps. The reluctance to close the door. The way the apartment felt different when he was in it, it wasn't because of anything he said or did, he was careful, but simply because the presence of another adult who was steady and reliable and made no demands. She did not dress it up as more than it was. She also did not pretend it was nothing.

She did not know yet what to do with something.

She turned back inside.

Emily was standing in front of the empty shelves with her arms crossed, her small face set in a look of absolute command.

"The chess box goes on the second shelf," she said. "So, I can reach it."

"Okay," Paige said.

She looked at her daughter. The straight back. The chin lifted. The absolute certainty about what she needed and where it belonged. Paige felt the familiar doubling, the love that had no edges, and underneath it something that was almost gratitude. Emily always knew what shelf the chess box went on. Emily always had a next thing. On the nights when Paige couldn't locate the next thing herself, Emily's certainty was what she navigated by.

Paige picked up her coffee.

It was completely cold but she drank it anyway.

She stood at the counter in her robe in the mid-morning quiet and she drank cold coffee and she looked at her daughter arranging chess pieces on a shelf she had decided was hers, and she thought about footsteps on a staircase, and she thought about her mother in a kitchen not unlike this one, and she thought about the passage between understanding something and being released by it, and she wondered, not for the first time and not with any expectation of an answer, how long the passage was and whether she was moving through it or simply standing at its entrance.

She finished the coffee.

She put the mug in the sink.

She went to help Emily with the shelf.

Marc Cianfarani

Chapter Twenty-Six

The warehouse ran hot in the afternoons, but today felt different. Jake had been sweating since the first hour; thin and cold despite the heat, soaking through his collar before the morning was half gone.

He told himself it was the humidity.

The beam was longer than Jake expected.

Louis took the front end without looking back, moving through the narrow aisle between stacked drywall sheets.

"Grab that side," he said.

Jake lifted the other end. The wood settled across his shoulder with a weight that pulls through his arms and into the familiar weak place behind his knee.

"Careful," Louis said. "Long load."

They step forward together.

The beam wobbled slightly as they turned the corner. Jake adjusted his grip, shifting the weight higher on his shoulder.

For a few steps everything held.

Then the knee slipped.

No sharp pain. The sudden absence of strength.

The beam dipped.

Louis jerked his end upward instinctively, the wood twisting between them, and then the geometry of the thing turned wrong all at once. Too much weight, wrong angle, nowhere for it to go except down.

Louis went with it.

He hit the concrete floor hard, the beam glancing

across his lower back before clattering sideways into the shelving. The sound of it was enormous in the narrow aisle. Metal on concrete. Wood splitting against steel.

Then Louis made a sound. The sound of pain.

Jake stood with his hands still raised where the beam had been, unable to move.

Around the corner, footsteps. Someone shouting. Then more footsteps.

"Louis…."

"Get the nurse…"

"Don't move him…"

Three workers appeared at the end of the aisle. Two more from the other direction. Someone was on a radio. Someone else crouched beside Louis with a hand on his shoulder saying his name steadily.

Louis was on the floor with his face turned sideways against the concrete, jaw tight. His breathing came in short controlled increments, the breathing of a man managing pain.

Jake looked at him. And then Jake was somewhere else.

Like the warehouse had become a photograph of itself and he was standing outside the frame looking in.

He knew that position. He had been in that position. The track beneath him and the grit on his cheek. The pain.

Someone was speaking to him but Jake did not register.

The manager stood beside him. He was not looking at Louis but was looking at Jake.

"Come with me," he said.

Jake went with him.

As they turned toward the office corridor, the manager glanced once toward the far end of the floor. A brief look with a slow motion of his head.

The security guard near the exit door straightened and fell into step twenty feet behind them.

The office was small and ordinary. Two chairs. A window that looked onto the parking lot rather than the floor.

The manager sat. Jake sat across from him.

Behind Jake, near the door, the security guard took up position without being asked. Jake did not turn around but he could feel him there.

The manager opened a folder. He did not look at it.

"Louis says the beam slipped," he said.

Jake nodded. "It wasn't bad when it happened," Jake said.

The manager paused. "His back…"

"I thought it would settle. That's what I kept thinking." Jake's voice was even, unhurried. "The doctors said the same thing at first. That sometimes these things settle."

The manager looked at him.

"You're talking about Louis."

Jake said nothing.

"He's with the nurse now. She's called the ambulance" He set the pen down. "This is a serious injury."

"I know what a serious injury is," Jake said.

It came out quietly.

The manager studied him.

"Are you on anything right now? Medication?"

The question landed and Jake heard it, but what came up in response to it was not the warehouse or the beam. What came up was a pharmacy counter at night. The weight of a decision made in a hurry.

"I went to get it," Jake said. "The pharmacy was three blocks. I thought she was asleep." He paused. "I thought I'd be back before she woke up."

The manager did not write anything this time. He was looking at Jake.

"Jake," he said.

"I had the prescription," Jake said. "I wasn't buying anything I wasn't supposed to have."

"Jake I'm asking about Today."

Jake looked at the desk between them. It was trying to come back into focus, but it wouldn't. "I take something for the knee," he said. "Before shifts sometimes. It helps me function."

"How long has this been going on?" The manager asked.

"I don't remember, but before Mexico."

The manager's pen stopped.

"Mexico," he repeated.

"The clinic said the nerve pathways needed…it doesn't matter." Jake pressed his palms flat against his thighs. "I was managing it."

The manager closed the folder.

He was quiet.

"Louis has a wife," the manager said. "Two kids."

"I know that," Jake said. "He told me."

The manager glanced at the security guard.

"That's why I'm here," Jake said. "That's the whole reason I'm here."

He wasn't talking about the warehouse. He wasn't talking about the beam or the shift he'd taken four months ago when Ms. Citino had led him off the bus and told the supervisor he was a hard worker.

He was talking about Paige and Emily.

The manager heard something else entirely.

He reached into his desk drawer and produced a small form. He slid it across the desk.

"I'm going to need your badge," he said.

Jake looked at the form.

"You were on probation for 6 months," the manager said. "I don't need a reason."

"Is this because of today?"

The manager said nothing.

Jake unpinned the badge from his jacket.

The walk was not long. Past the supply station. Past the cable rack. Men looked up. Some of them. The ones looked up understood immediately what the escort meant. Jake could see the Paramedics exiting the building with Louis in a stretcher.

The noise of the floor returned to normal. Forklifts and machines were running again. At the corridor near the main exit, a door was propped open. The administrative wing. Through it, Jake could see the row of offices.

Ms. Citino was coming out of it. She was carrying the thermos she always carried. She was mid-step when she saw him. She saw the security guard first. Then Jake's face.

Her hand rose to cover her mouth. She did not look away.

Jake held her gaze for one step. Two.

Then the exit door opened in front of him.

Jake sat on the edge of the bed afterward, phone in hand. The room feels unfinished without Paige's things. He considers calling her but doesn't.

Days stretch. Jake sells the old speakers. Then the bike he hasn't ridden since before the injury.

Some afternoons he walks the park near the apartment. He sits on the same bench, watching people pass, parents going for walk, kids on scooters. He notices how no one looks at anyone else for very long.

One evening, Paige texts.

"We're okay. Wanted you to know."

He reads it three times.

"I'm glad", he types.

She doesn't reply.

Jake lies on the couch that night, staring at the ceiling, listening to the building settle around him. He tries to remember the last time he felt urgency.

Jake misses a payment. Then another. The notices come in thin envelopes he stops opening. He stacks them by the door.

The landlord leaves a voicemail, polite, firm. Jake deletes it without listening to the end. He knows how it finishes. A second voicemail comes three days later. Less polite. More certain. Jake doesn't delete that one. He doesn't listen. A third arrives the following week.

He can tell from the length of it, that there are no

more courtesies left inside.

One afternoon he's sitting on the couch, staring at nothing in particular, when he hears it.

A sound at the front door. Metal on metal. The soft, methodical turning of a screwdriver.

He gets up, crosses the room, pulls the door open.

A man in uniform stands in the hallway, a toolbox at his feet, the lock plate half-removed from the doorframe. He looks up without surprise.

"What's going on?" Jake asks.

The man straightens. His voice is steady, not unkind.

"Here to enforce the eviction notice, sir. Court order came through this morning."

Jake looks at the lock. At the man. At the hallway that suddenly feels narrower than it ever has.

"I'm sorry."

The words come out before he can stop them.

"I've found myself in a really bad situation. I just. I need this place. For when Emily comes back. My daughter. She's coming back with her mother and this is our home."

The deputy holds his gaze.

"I'm sorry," he says. "There's nothing I can do. You have to leave the premises now."

Jake stands there. He turns back inside. He moves fast. His mind hasn't caught up yet.

He grabs the backpack from the closet, opens it wide, starts pulling things from shelves and drawers without a system. Socks. A clean shirt. A jacket he probably doesn't need. The photograph of Emily is on the windowsill. Her face smeared with a purple streak and laughing uncontrollably. He glances at it. Keeps moving.

His old running shoes are by the door. He holds them, feeling the worn flat of the sole, then puts them down. He doesn't take them. He's not thinking clearly and he knows that. He takes things he won't need and leaves things he will. There isn't time for clarity. When he comes back to the doorway, the deputy is waiting.

"Sorry," Jake says again, quieter this time. "For the trouble."

The deputy gives a small nod.

"Take care of yourself."

Jake steps into the hallway. He doesn't look back.

Outside, he makes it to the end of the block before he stops walking. He sits on a low concrete step outside a dry cleaner's, backpack between his feet, and tries to breathe.

Tries to think. Tries to remember what he took and what he left. He opens the bag. Digs to the bottom. Checks the side pocket. Nothing.

"Emily's picture." He says it out loud, barely a whisper, like saying it might make it appear.

He's on his feet before he decides to move, backpack swinging over one shoulder, walking fast, then faster, back the way he came. The knee protests. He ignores it.

The building door is unlocked. He takes the stairs.

When he reaches his floor, he stops. The door to his apartment is shut. The new lock catches the light, brighter than the old one, still clean. A small sticker on the handle he doesn't read.

The deputy is gone.

Jake knocks. Three times. Firm.

Waits.

Nothing.

He knocks again, harder this time.

Waits.

Silence.

He presses his forehead lightly against the door, with his eyes closed.

He can picture exactly where the photograph is.

Window sill. Right side. Corner curling up slightly where the sun caught it. He stands there longer than he should. He picks up the backpack, turns around, and walks back down the stairs. As he steps into the street a thought arrives.

Just get through today.

Chapter Twenty-Seven

The building door closed behind him and Jake kept walking. He had his jacket. His phone and forty-three dollars with some change in his front pocket. His key was still in his other pocket. He didn't throw it away. His legs didn't stop.

The street was ordinary. That was the strangest part. The city hadn't registered what had happened. A woman walked a dog on the opposite sidewalk, the dog pulling toward a fire hydrant, the woman scrolling her phone without looking up. A delivery truck sat double-parked with its hazards blinking. None of it paused.

Jake turned left because the light was green.

Then right because the block ahead looked the same as the one behind him.

He walked for a long time without counting the streets or checking direction. The city thinned gradually, storefronts giving way to older buildings, older buildings giving way to the long dark stretch of a park he recognized. He had run here before, in a different life, on legs that hadn't yet learned what failure felt like.

He found a bench set back from the path, half-hidden under the wide spread of an oak that hadn't fully shed yet. He sat and he put his elbows on his knees and looked at the ground between his shoes.

He told himself he would think through his options.

At some point, without meaning to, he lay down. He used his jacket as a pillow because his neck ached and the armrest was pressing into the wrong place. He looked up at the tree above him, the branches black against a sky that was never fully dark in the city, always that dull amber wash from the streetlights.

His eyes closed.

Sleep came faster than expected.

He woke and didn't know where he was.

It wasn't the gentle confusion of walking in an unfamiliar hotel or a friend's couch. A hard surface. A full body blankness that lasted two, maybe three seconds, in which he was no one, nowhere, without history or address or name.

Then his hip registered the bench slat beneath it. Then the cold arrived all at once. His shoulders then the back of his neck where the collar of his jacket had shifted.

He sat up.

The park was dark and absolutely quiet, the kind that only exists between two and four in the morning. The path was deserted. Somewhere distant a car passed on a road he couldn't see. Jake sat with his hands between his knees and looked at the path.

His brain tried to assemble a morning. A routine. Some version of what happened next. It reached for the shape of a day, making coffee in the kitchen, observing the particular light through the window above the sink but he found nothing to hold onto.

He had nowhere to be in the morning. No one waiting for him to come through a door.

He pressed his palms flat against the bench slat. The wood was cold and faintly damp, textured with small ridges of peeling paint. He pressed harder without meaning to.

He was still here.

He reached into his pocket. His phone screen in front of his face, pale and clinical. 3:17am. The battery was at eleven percent. He had four unread messages, that he hadn't opened in two days and three missed calls.

He turned the screen over against his thigh.

The dark came back.

Above him, through the branches, the sky was the color that couldn't decide between night and morning. He looked at it like you look at things you stopped noticing years ago, the sky had been there, background. He had not actually looked at it longer than he could remember. It reminded him of when he was 11 or 12 running outside with his friends. Sometimes, when it got dark at night, they would lie on the grass and stare at the sky, the stars and wonder what was up there. He hadn't done that since then.

He looked at it now.

A plane moved across the gap between the branches, red light blinking at steady intervals, impossibly high. Jake watched it until is disappeared.

His knee ached with the dull insistence it had lately, not sharp, present.

He thought about Paige. The version of her from a long time ago, standing at the edge of a soccer field with a notebook tucked under her arm, saying you're going to call him like she could see the shape of his future better than he did. Her voice had been certain without being unkind. He wondered if she could see this.

He pressed the heels of his hands against his eyes and held them there until the darkness behind his eyelids developed its own dim patterns. In through the nose. Out through the mouth. Jake lowered his hands. The park was still there. He was not going to solve anything tonight. Tonight was for getting through. He lay back down. He pulled his jacket tighter across his shoulders and tucked his chin and drew his knee up slightly against the cold. He closed his eyes, but did not sleep for a long time.

The next morning, Jake took the bus to the city. He wasn't going to go to the University but the downtown area he was familiar with that housed a few shelters.

He had left Cottage Grove before heading north with a card in his pocket and a future he could almost see. Now he was leaving again, heading back to the city that had taken everything because at least that city had somewhere for a man to sleep.

That evening he made his way to the shelter.

The shelter intake desk was manned by a middle-aged man with a blue uniform and a name tag. Jake stood at the back of a short line, backpack on both shoulders.

He didn't know how any of it worked. That was the first thing. He didn't know you needed ID. He didn't know there was a cutoff time, or that beds were first-come, and that first-come meant people who had been doing this long enough to know when to show up. He didn't know that the intake form asked questions he didn't have clean answers to, permanent address, emergency contact, last place of employment, questions that had once been easy.

The man behind the desk looked tired, the kind that comes form doing three people's jobs. He moved through the questions quickly, without space for hesitation.

"ID," he said.

Jake produced his driver's license. Expired by two months. The man looked at it, then at Jake, then made a notation on a form.

"Any weapons, controlled substances?"

"No."

"Medical condition I should know about?"

Jake thought about the knee. "No," he said.

The man handed him a laminated card with a number on it and pointed down the hall. "Locker's in there. Keep your valuables on you. Lights out at ten. Breakfast at six-thirty, you have to be in line by six-fifteen or it's gone."

Jake nodded as if he'd understood all of it.

He hadn't understood most of it.

The bunk room held twenty men. The smell was human and close and layered; sweat, damp fabric, medicinal from the far corner. Bare bulbs overhead. Two narrow windows set high on the wall, the kind designed to let in light without letting anyone see out or in.

Jake found his assigned number, a lower bunk near the middle of the room. He sat on the edge of it. The mattress was thin and the plastic cover crinkled under his weight. The man in the bunk above him didn't look down.

He put his backpack on the floor between his feet.

Immediately the man across the aisle spoke. He was short and slender, maybe mid-forties but wearing every one of those years twice over. He sat on the edge of his bunk with his hands loose in his lap and when he looked at Jake his eyes were unlike anything Jake had ever seen; red that went beyond tired, deep chemical red that didn't belong in a human face. And there was a smell coming off him. It wan't body odor. Sharper, industrial. The best Jake could come up with was turpentine. Though that wasn't quite it, more like whatever turpentine was trying to be before it gave up and became worse.

"Don't put it there." The man said.

Jake looked up.

"Under your pillow end. Or on the bunk with you."

"Thanks," Jake said.

The man nodded once. "Pal," he said.

Jake moved the bag. "Jake"

Pal turned back to the wall without further ceremony, as the introduction had used up exactly as much energy as he'd budgeted for.

Jake lay down with his shoes still on. He wasn't sure if that was allowed. Nobody told him either way. Around him, men settled into their own routines, some asleep, some reading on phones with cracked screens, one man praying in a language Jake didn't recognize. The room had a rhythm to it that everyone else seemed to know.

Jake stared at the underside of the bunk above him and tried to sleep. He was almost there when he heard it.

A quiet, deliberate rustling. The unmistakable sound of someone going through a bag that wasn't theirs.

He sat up.

A young guy, maybe twenty, was crouched at the foot of a bunk two down, hands inside someone's duffel. The duffel's owner was asleep. The young guy moved quickly and practiced, fingers probing without disturbing.

He didn't notice Jake watching.

Jake sat up. His first instinct was to find the night staff.

It took four minutes. The staffer came back with him, flashlight in hand, matter-of-fact. The young guy was gone by then. The duffel's owner was awake now, confused, patting his bag. The staffer made a note. Said he'd look into it.

Jake went back to his bunk.

He didn't understand what he'd done wrong until the lights went out. Then the whispers started. The low murmur of a room recalibrating around him. He caught fragments. The gist was clear. He'd gone to staff. He'd named a name. In here, that was a rule you learned before any other.

You didn't do that.

He lay rigid in the dark and felt the temperature of the room change.

In the morning, his shoes were gone.

He knew before he reached down. He could tell from the silence in the room, and how nobody looked at him and nobody looked away. He sat on the edge of the bunk in his socked feet and understood what the night had cost him.

He went to the desk.

"Someone took my shoes."

The woman at the morning shift wrote it down. "You can check the lost and found. We can't monitor belongings overnight."

Outside the bunk room, the man from the night before, the one who had told him to move his bag, was pulling on a jacket near the exit. He glanced at Jake's feet. Then at Jake's face. He gave a small shake of his head. Not contempt.

"Not safe for you here tonight," he said. "Word travels."

He walked out without further explanation.

Jake stood in the hallway in his socks.

A sign near the stairwell read Health Services-Ground Floor. An arrow pointed left. He wasn't sure what made him follow it. The knee, probably. It had been on a plastic mattress all night and it was letting him know.

The room at the end of the corridor was small, partitioned off with a curtain on a rod. A woman sat behind a narrow desk. Clipboard, coffee bedside her keyboard. She didn't look up when he came in.

"Sit," she said.

He sat in the plastic chair against the wall.

She finished what she was writing, then looked at him.

"What do you need?"

"My knee," Jake said.

She came around the desk and crouched in front of him, pressed two fingers along the joint. He kept his face still.

"Does that hurt?"

"It's manageable."

She stood. "Any prescriptions currently?"

Jake paused.

"I used to," he said.

She went to the back behind the desk, opened the bottom drawer and produced two aspirin in a small paper cup. She set them on the corner of the desk closest to him.

"Fountain is in the hall," she said and turned back to her clipboard.

Jake took the cup.

"Thank you," he said.

He took the aspirin standing at fountain, alone in the corridor. The water was cold and he held it in his mouth a second before swallowing. He straightened and stood there a moment, the empty cap still in his hand.

He didn't know what he'd expected her to give him. Something that would hold until whatever came next. But there was nothing available. This was the bottom of what the system could offer a man with an expired ID and no address.

Two aspirin in a paper cup.

He dropped it in the bin by the fountain and walked back down the hall.

Near the exit, a donation bin held folded clothing, a pair of boots with mismatched laces, and at the bottom, a pair of canvas shoes. He dug them out. Too big by at least a size.

He put them on anyway and walked into the morning.

He didn't go back.

Marc Cianfarani

Chapter Twenty-Eight

The park he wanted was on the wrong side of an invisible line. He didn't know that yet. It felt safer than the alleys near the intake center where he understood his face was known and not favorably. The park had trees. It had a stone retaining wall under an overhang wall on the eastern side that blocked the wind and a stretch of bench under an overhang that stayed dry when it rained.

He pushed his cart in at dusk, found a spot, and started to settle.

Three men appeared from the direction of the trees. They didn't rush but they walked the way people walk when they aren't worried about outcome. The one in front was heavyset, wearing a military surplus jacket repaired at the collar with electrical tape. He stopped about ten feet from Jake and looked at the cart, then at Jake, then at the cart again.

"This isn't where you sleep," he said.

Jake looked around. "There's no one here."

"There's us," the man said.

The two behind didn't speak. One was young, maybe late twenties, with a stillness that was harder to read then the heavyset man's directness. The other was older, leaning against a tree with arms crossed, watching the path behind Jake as much as he was watching Jake himself.

"I don't want any trouble," Jake said.

"Then you know what to do." The heavyset man

nodded toward the path Jake had come in on.

Jake's hands tightened on the cart. He felt the old heat rise, the same reflex that used to carry him off the starting line before his brain fully engaged. He recognized it. For once, he didn't follow it.

He picked up the cart and left. He walked two blocks before he let himself stop. His heart was loud. His feet, still in the too big canvas shoes, had raised a blister on his left heel. He sat on a low wall outside a closed laundromat and tried to think.

He didn't hear the footsteps until they were close.

He turned fast.

The older man from the group stood at the edge of the laundromat's awning. He stood inside the light of the awning, rooted there, making it clear the sidewalk wasn't as empty as it looked. There, watching Jake.

Jake stood. "I left."

"I know," the man said. "I followed you."

Ray didn't blink; he waited for Jake to realize he wasn't leaving.

"Why?" Jake asked.

The man tilted his head slightly. He was maybe sixty, the thing that came from years of walking instead of riding. He had close-cropped grey hair and a face that had been outdoors long enough to forget what indoors felt like. His eyes were steady.

"You don't know how any of this works," the man said.

Jake didn't argue with it.

"I watched you at the park. How you came in. How you set up." He paused. "You put your cart perpendicular to the wall. Somebody taught you that or you worked it out?"

"Worked it out," Jake said.

The man nodded. "My name's Ray."

Jake hesitated. "Jake."

Ray looked at him a moment longer, then turned and started walking. He didn't look back to see if jake followed. Jake followed.

They didn't talk for two blocks. Ray moved at a deliberate pace. He took alleys Jake wouldn't have chosen, crossed streets at angles that kept them out of sightlines Jake hadn't thought to map. It was like watching someone navigate a city that existed on no map available to Jake.

"Army?" Jake asked finally.

"Marines," Ray said. "Two tours. Came back to a VA that was working on it." A short exhale. "Took about five years for working on it to catch up to me."

Jake said nothing.

"You?" Ray asked.

"Runner. College. Blew my knee senior year." Jake looked at Ray. "Things fell apart after."

Ray glanced at him sidelong. "They do that."

He stopped at a recessed off a side street, deep enough to break the wind, shallow enough to see the sidewalk in both directions. A flattened piece of cardboard lay on the ground. A folded blanket on top. A small battery lantern with the light turned low.

"First thing," Ray said, sitting and gesturing for Jake to take the wall beside him. "The park you want, Deacon and his group have had that section for two winters.

That's long enough that it's theirs. Doesn't matter what the law says. You go in there again without an understanding, you'll have more than a conversation.

"What understanding?"

"You ask," Ray said. "You don't ask for permission. But for a reason they can say yes to. Deacon's not unreasonable. He's territorial and he's been burned before by people who came in and made things harder for everyone." He looked at Jake. "You from here originally?"

"Cottage Grove," replied Jake.

"That's part of it. New face, no context. He doesn't know what you are yet."

"What am I?"

Ray considered that. "Don't know yet," he said honestly. "But you didn't punch back at the park, and you didn't follow us to see where we slept. That counts."

They sat while the city moved past the mouth of the doorway, distant traffic, a siren, the clank of a gate somewhere down the block.

"The shelter," Jake said. "Last night. I reported someone going through another guy's bag and …"

"And your shoes were gone in the morning," Ray finished.

Jake looked at him.

"It's the first thing everyone does." Ray said. Not unkindly. "You came from a world where you report things. Where there's structure and structure is supposed to fix it. In there, the structure can't protect you and everyone knows it, so you protect yourself. You go to staff, and you've announced that you don't understand the rules. That make you unsafe to be around."

"So, someone gets to go through bags."

"No," Ray said. "You handle it yourself. Quietly. Or you let it go and move your bag." He paused. "There's a version where you say it directly to the man doing it. That has its own risk. But it keeps it inside the room."

Jake absorbed this. It ran against every instinct he had, for fairness, for authority.

"It's not fair," he said.

"No," Ray agreed. "You accept it."

Ray turned to look at him fully. "You accept what you can't change tonight. You change what you can tomorrow."

Ray reached into the side of his pack and produced two bread rolls in a paper sleeve. He held one out. Jake took it.

"Garbage bins behind restaurants," Ray said. "Best time, is after eleven on weekdays. Weekends are hit or miss. Too much competition and the restaurants are more careful. Bakeries are morning, before six, before the staff arrives. Coffee shops mid-morning after the rush they throw out a lot. Grocery loading docks, Tuesdays and Thursdays."

He said it like a coach explains a training schedule.

Jake ate the roll and listened.

"Bathrooms. Library on Fifth, stays open until eight. Red center on Marwood has a door code, it's been the same for two years because nobody's bothered to change it, but don't advertise that. Gas station on Clement will let you use the key if you buy a small item. A coffee. Worth it."

"Worst spots?"

Ray considered. "Anywhere with new security. Anywhere near the courthouse. The overpass on Western is good cover but the city sweeps it every third week and they don't give notice anymore." He paused. "And anywhere Deacon's group has been long enough to call home. It isn't because they're violent. Because stress makes things go wrong and you don't need that right now."

Jake nodded.

They sat in silence. The lantern threw a soft pool of light across the cardboard. Jake's shoes were starting to dry from the walk.

"You going to be all right?" Ray asked.

Jake thought. "I don't know," he said.

Ray nodded. "That's the right answer."

He reached into his pack and produced a pair of thick wool socks. He set them on the ground between them.

"Church on Alderman gives them out Tuesday mornings," he said. "Get there before eight."

Jake picked them up. He held them.

"Why?" Jake asked.

Ray looked at him.

"Why are you helping me."

Ray was quiet. Then: "I watched you leave that park without a fight. A man who does that still has his head." He paused. "But you're still looking."

He picked up the lantern and turned it off.

"I'll see you around." said Ray, as he left walking in the direction they had started from.

Jake lay down on the hard ground with the wall at his back. He thought about the park. He thought about Deacon and about the idea of an understanding. He thought about what Ray had said.

He closed his eyes.

The next morning, his phone stopped lighting up. No warning. No final vibration. A blank screen that didn't respond. He tried the power button. Held it. Released. Nothing. He asked at a corner shop if there was a charger he could borrow. The clerk shook his head before Jake finished the sentence.

Outside, Jake checked the screen again. A small notice flashed when it finally woke: Service suspended. He stood there longer than necessary, thumb hovering.

He walked to a trash can and dropped it in. The sound was dull. Final. Without the phone, time loosened. Days blurred at the edges. No calls. No missed calls. No numbers to remember.

He walked when the stiffness settled in his knee. Stopped when it didn't. The pain flattened. It was constant, no longer demanding attention. One afternoon, he passed a track without meaning to. The gate was open. Kids ran drills under a coach's whistle. The sound cut through him.

He kept walking.

Chapter Twenty-Nine

Over time a route took shape along the river path toward the Whitaker district, under the Douglas firs where the track team used to run Sundays. Jake followed without thinking. It always began behind the bakery, at the row of disposal bins where they tossed day-old bread and the pastries that didn't sell. If he got there before sunrise, before the employees arrived, he could sometimes find it, still wrapped, still good.

This morning, he found nothing.

He moved on, continuing along the routes he'd traced across the city, alleys, loading docks, quiet spots behind coffee shops. Near the end of his route sat a burger place with sprawling outdoor patio. He timed it for early lunch, when customers ate quickly and staff hadn't yet begun clearing the tables.

Half the patio sat empty. Jake scanned the tables from a distance, the wrappers, cups, napkins, the small messes people left behind. He saw it.

Half a burger.

He moved toward it without rushing, sat, unwrapped it, and ate in small careful bites.

A few tables ahead, a woman and her daughter arrived. The woman sat with her back to him. The girl, five maybe six faced him directly. She noticed him first. Her eyes lit.

She smiled, lifted a small hand and waved, first with her right hand and then with both her hands at the same time.

Jake froze, a piece of bun still between his fingers. He hadn't been waved at in a long time. He lifted his hand and waved back.

The woman turned at the motion. Her expression tightened. She pulled her daughter close and walked her inside

Jake lowered his hand and let it rest on the table.

The manager approached, with a heavy, practiced weariness. He looked past Jake toward the street. "We've got a lunch rush coming, man. You gotta move."

Jake nodded. He stood, tossed the wrapper, and walked away. He kept walking until the noise of the patio faded, replaced by the hum of traffic. Finally, he sat on the sidewalk, back against a retaining wall, hands folded loosely in his lap.

The little girl's wave stayed with him. Both hands, like Emily always did it.

Later that day, footsteps slowed beside him.

"Hey," a young voice said; gentle, careful.

Jake looked up. A teenager stood there, maybe sixteen or seventeen, a volunteer badge hanging from a frayed lanyard. He held a coffee in one hand and a folded blanket in the other.

"You want these?" The boy asked. "It's nothing fancy."

Jake hesitated. The kid didn't look away.

"I'm good." Jake said finally.

"There's a shelter close by," the boy offered. "They've got beds tonight."

Jake shook his head.

"All right."

But the boy didn't leave.

"Anything I can do?" he said. "I mean… even something small?"

Jake thought about it.

Then, surprising himself, he said.

"Do you ... have a phone?"

The boy brightened. "Yeah, of course."

He pulled it out immediately. "You want me to call someone?"

Before Jake could answer, two men in suits walked past on the sidewalk.

"Christ, what's that smell?" One muttered.

"Whole area's getting like this," the other replied. "City needs to start cleaning these bums off the street."

Jake heard every word. His jaw tightened.

The boy noticed.

"Hey," the boy said, "Ignore them."

He offered the phone again.

Jake looked in the direction the men had gone, then back at the screen reflecting his own face. He looked tired, older than he remembered. He shook his head.

"No. It's okay."

The boy nodded. Jake leaned against the wall again, eyes unfocused. The moment passed.

The night had teeth. Jake pulled the tarp tighter across the opening and pressed himself against the base of the trees, knees drawn in, the cold working its way through every layer he owned.

He shifted his feet, feeling the thin crinkle around them, the unused dog-waste bags he'd slipped over his socks earlier, ones found along the trail. They weren't warm. They kept the damp out, and sometimes that was the difference between losing feeling and holding on to it. He curled his toes, testing what little warmth remained.

He reached into the cart and pulled out the folded newspapers he'd gathered that afternoon. Someone had showed him, you layer them inside the jacket, close to the skin, trapping whatever warmth your body makes. He'd been skeptical the first time.

Not anymore. He smoothed the first sheet open across his chest. His hands moved automatically, folding, pressing, working by feel in the near dark. He didn't read them. He slid a second page beneath his jacket. Then stopped.

A photograph. Large. Centered. Even in the dim light bleeding in from the path lamps, it was impossible not to see.

FORMER SPRINGFIELD STAR MAKES OLYMPIC TEAM

Mitch stood in the middle of the frame, taller than the people around him, shoulders squared, jaw set in that familiar way, controlled, victorious without trying to look like it. He's holding a small flag. The smile is modest. Earned.

Behind him, slightly out of focus, Paige stands with Emily on her hip. They're smiling. They were not aware of the camera. But present, caught mid-moment.

Jake doesn't move. The cold kept coming. His eyes traced details he wished he couldn't see: Emily's hair pulled back clumsily, the strap of Paige's bag digging into her shoulder, Mitch's hand resting lightly at Emily's back, not possessive, certain.

He reads the article twice.

It's clean. Celebratory. It mentioned discipline, perseverance, second chances. Quotes Mitch on gratitude and support systems. There's a line about family near the end. Paige's name appears there, briefly, naturally, as if it belonged.

No mention of Jake. There wouldn't be.

He kept the page pressed to his chest.

This isn't betrayal, he told himself. There's no villainy in the wording. No theft. Time moving forward. He stayed still.

When he finally moved, he didn't fold it back. He didn't set it aside. He held it there, the photograph turned inward.

Sleep doesn't come. The image stays.

His chest pulled tight. He exhales, like he used to before races. In through the nose. Out through the mouth. Count it. Control it.

At first, it's nothing, breath shaped oddly in the cold. Then it steadies, finds a pitch.

A hum. The lullaby. You are my sunshine.

The one he used to hum when Emily wouldn't settle. Low and quiet so Paige could sleep. Tuneless on purpose, like if he didn't care about it, it couldn't be taken from him.

The sound wavers. His throat tightens. Tears come without permission, hot and sudden, blurring what little dark he can see. He presses his lips together, but the hum continues, breaking, reforming.

Eventually it fades, replaced by the wind through branches. Jake leans his head against the tree and stares

Marc Cianfarani

into the dark.

Chapter Thirty

The kitchen smelled like the blueberry pancakes Paige had made for Emily.

Emily sat at the table now, the plate pushed to one side, a card in front of her. Purple and yellow construction paper, her best handwriting across the front.

Happy Father's Day.

Paige saw it from the doorway and felt the air leave the room.

She had known this was coming. She had been knowing it was coming for years now, the way Emily had begun asking questions that stopped just short of the question she actually wanted to ask. Paige had been preparing her answers and finding them insufficient and preparing them again. She had rehearsed this conversation in the shower and on the drive to school and in the thirty second between turning off the bedroom light and sleep arriving. She had never found a version of it that didn't cost something.

She came in and sat across from her daughter.

Emily didn't look up right away.

Her fingers traced the edge of the card the like she did when she was thinking, the same gesture she made over chess pieces when she was deciding, the same internal   stillness that Paige had watched develop in her across the last two years and that she recognized something Emily had build deliberately, a way of being in her own body that didn't betray what was happening inside it. She learned this somewhere. Paige did not like knowing where.

"Who's that for?" Paige asked, even though she knew.

Emily looked up.

"You know who it's for."

Paige set her coffee down.

"Em."

"I want to send it to him." Emily's voice was measured.

"I need an address."

Paige opened her mouth, then stopped. She looked at her daughter across the kitchen table and felt the full weight of what she was about to say and what it was going to cost Emily to hear it and what it was going to cost her to watch Emily hear it She had known this moment was coming and the knowing had not prepared her for the reality of it, her daughter's face across a kitchen table on a Sunday morning with a purple and yellow card and her best handwriting and the complete expectation that her mother would have an address.

"I don't have an address, baby."

Emily stared at her. "Why not?"

"Because I don't know where he is."

The steadiness in Emily's face cracked slightly.

"Did you try?" Emily asked. "To find him?"

"Yes" no hesitation. That much Paige could give her without flinching.

"Yes. I tried."

"How?"

"I called people. Friends from school. His old teammates. People who knew him."

Paige kept her voice even. She was performing the steadiness she did not feel because Emily needed to be able to ask the questions and she could not ask them if Paige was falling apart across the table. This was the calculation she had been making for two years. Emily's access to the truth versus Emily's need for a mother who was not destroyed by the truth. She had been trying to give her both and she was not certain she had succeeded and she was not certain it was possible

"I left messages, I asked around."

Emily absorbed this.

"And nobody knew?"

A silence opened up between them.

"Did he know about me?" Emily asked.

"Before he left. Did he know I existed?"

"He knew," she said. "He loved you. Very much."

"Then why"

"I don't know, Em." She steadied herself.

"I've asked myself that a thousand times and I don't have a good answer. Sometimes people get lost in ways that don't make sense from the outside."

Emily looked down at the card.

Her thumb pressed against the corner, bending it slightly then smoothing it flat again.

"Is he alive?" she asked.

Paige had prepared for many versions of this conversation across many imagined nights. She thought about what she actually knew.

She had called his old number two years ago and gotten a disconnected tone. She had called two of his former teammates and left messages that were never returned. She called Ms. Citino who told her about what happened with his job and that she had not seen him and he no longer lived at the apartment. Paige had searched his name online and found nothing after a certain point, no trail, no trace, the digital absence of a person who had stopped existing.

She didn't know if he was alive.

She had not allowed herself to finish that thought all the way to its conclusion. She finished it now, sitting across from the daughter who needed the truth more than she needed to be protected from it.

"I don't know," Paige said.

Emily didn't cry immediately.

She nodded once, very slightly, as if it confirmed what she'd hoped wasn't true.

Then her face crumpled.

It wasn't loud. Emily had never been a loud crier. She bent forward over the card, shoulders pulling in, and the sound she made was small. Paige was around the table before she thought about moving. She pulled Emily against her, one hand cradling the back of her head, and said nothing.

She pressed her lips to her daughter's hair and held on.

She thought about Jake.

The one from the ball pit photograph. The one who held Emily in the delivery room. She thought about him somewhere in the city, in the state she had left, or not in the city or state, she didn't know, she genuinely did not know, and she felt the grief of that not knowing move through her while she held their daughter and she let it move through her because there was nowhere else for it to go.

Emily cried until she went quiet.

She pulled back enough to look at her mother's face.

Her eyes were swollen dry now. Thoughtful.

"I have another one." Emily said.

Paige blinked. "What?"

Emily slid off the chair and left the kitchen. Her footsteps moved down the hall. A drawer opened. Closed.

She came back holding a small stack of construction paper cards, edges soft from handling, corners bent from being taken out and put away more than once.

She set them on the table.

Paige stared.

Three cards. Purple, yellow, green, red. The handwriting changed across them. So did the drawings.

Happy Father's Day

Happy Father's Day

Happy Father's Day

Paige pressed her hand flat against the table.

"Emily."

"I don't know where to send them. So, I kept them," Emily said simply.

She looked at the cards and understood what she was looking at. Three years of a child sitting at a table or desk or floor with construction paper and crayons and the absolute private intention of reaching someone she had no address for. Three years of making the thing anyway. Three years of keeping it in a drawer because the keeping was the only version of the sending available to her.

She thought about what is had cost Emily to keep this private.

Paige pulled Emily back into her arms and this time she was the one who cried.

Emily let her.

She reached up and patted her mother's arm with a steady hand.

"It's okay, Mom," she said softly.

Paige held her daughter and cried and felt the specific quality of being comforted by the person you were supposed to be comforting, the reversal of it, the way it was both unbearable and exactly right, like Emily's hand on her arm was the most adult thing she had ever felt from her child and the most heartbreaking.

Later, after Emily had gone to her room.

Paige sat alone at the kitchen table.

The cards were still there. She didn't move them. She sat with them spread in front of her, reading each one.

The drawings got better over the years. Stick figures gave way to more careful and detailed ones. In one, a man and a small girl run side by side. Emily had drawn them the same height.

She looked at that one for a long time.

She thought about the drawer. The decision Emily had made every year to add another card to the drawer rather than throw the previous year's away. The accumulated weight of that. Three cards in a drawer was not a child who had given up. It was a child who had refused to. Who had kept making the gesture even when the gesture had nowhere to go, because the making of it meant she wasn't willing to surrender.

Paige thought about surrender.

She thought about what she had surrendered and what she hadn't and where the line was between letting go of something because holding it was destroying you and letting go of something because you had stopped believing it was worth the cost of holding. She had told herself for two years that she was doing the former. Sitting at this table with three Father's Day cards in front of her and her daughter's handwriting changing across them she was less certain of the distinction.

She was not certain of very much tonight.

She picked up the card on top. The earliest one. The handwriting large and effortful, the letters slightly uneven.

At the bottom of that one, in her most recent handwriting.

I hope you come back. I save these for you.

Paige sat with that sentence. She had been telling herself for two years that she had made her peace with not knowing. That the not knowing was something she had accepted and organized her life around and that the organization was a kind of peace even if it wasn't the kind she would have chosen. She sat with her daughter's sentence and understood that the peace she had been describing to herself was not peace. It was management. It was the discipline her mother had modeled and she had inherited and she had been practicing so long she had mistaken it for resolution.

She had not resolved anything.

She was a woman sitting at a kitchen table and a daughter asleep down the hall who had been keeping faith with a man who had disappeared, and she did not know if he was alive, and she did not know what to do with any of it, and for the first time in two years she let herself not know without immediately reaching for the management of not knowing.

She sat in it.

The kitchen was quiet. The cards were in front of her.

She kept them company until Emily woke up.

Chapter Thirty-One

The auditorium smelled of floor wax and old curtain fabric. Paige found a seat in the fourth row, on the aisle, leaving one beside her empty.

Around her, families arranged themselves. Fathers with phones out. Grandmothers in good blouses. Younger siblings acting out.

She set her bag on the empty seat beside her.

The lights hadn't dimmed yet. On the stage, the velvet curtain hung still and thick and dark blue and behind it, Paige could hear the muffled shuffle and whisper of twenty-three third graders trying and failing to be quiet. She smiled. Emily would be in the back left. She always positioned herself back left, visible enough to be found, far enough not to be crowded.

Her phone buzzed.

"Running five minutes late. Save me a seat."

She looked at the empty chair beside her and moved her bag back to the floor.

Mitch arrived, sliding into the seat as the house lights began to dim. He was carrying flowers. A small bunch of yellow ones, wrapped in paper, slightly crushed from being held in one hand while he navigated the crowd.

"Sorry," he said under his breath.

"You made it," Paige said.

He held out the flowers.

Paige looked at him.

"Emily told me last week," he said. "That she was supposed to be a fox. That she changed her mind."

Paige laughed. "She didn't tell me that part."

The curtain opened.

The Christmas play was, in execution, somewhat chaotic. A snowman had lost his hat. Two of the elves appeared to be in a disagreement that predated the performance. Mrs. Claus was managing the situation with focused energy. The music teacher played the opening notes and the children snapped to attention with fierce concentration.

Paige found Emily immediately.

Back left. Of course.

She was dressed as the Grinch.

Green face applied with great thoroughness. A crooked felt hat. An expression of absolute contempt that made the woman two seats down press her hand to her mouth to keep from laughing out loud.

Emily found her.

Then found Mitch.

A look crossed her face, quick, complicated, private, then she was back to performing, entirely the Grinch.

Paige felt it too.

She didn't look at Mitch.

The play moved through its pieces. Santa arrived. The reindeers moved across the stage in a line that was almost straight.

And then it was Emily's turn.

She stepped forward with the unhurried confidence of someone who had decided exactly what she was going to do. She looked at the audience.

"I hate Christmas," she said.

Laughter from the audience. Warm, delighted.

"I hate gifts."

More laughter. A father near the back started recording.

"I hate all of this."

She gestured broadly at the stage, at Santa, at the elves, at the entire cheerful enterprise of it. The audience was fully with her now, laughing, leaning forward.

Then Emily's voice dropped, quieter, more considered. The comic rhythm broke without warning.

"Santa doesn't come to every home."

The laughter softened.

Some people smiled, uncertain whether this was still the bit.

Some people stopped smiling.

Paige sat very still.

Beside her, Mitch didn't move either.

He didn't look at Paige.

Emily held the beat for exactly one second. Then her chin came up, the contempt returned and she moved on the next line as though nothing had happened. Total composure. The performance continuing.

The audience laughed again, relieved.

Paige exhaled.

The performance ran twenty-two minutes. Emily

sang every word, hit every mark and took her bow with gravity that earned genuine laughter from the audience.

Afterward, in the corridor the children came flooding out through a side door into a press of waiting families. Emily spotted them.

She hugged Paige first. Long and tight.

Then she looked at Mitch.

He held out the flowers.

"You were the best Grinch," he said.

Emily considered this, "I know," she said, and took the flowers.

A woman nearby, another mother, someone Paige half recognized, glanced over at the three of them and smiled.

Paige saw the smile and understood what it was reading. A family. The configuration of it, a man and a woman and a child in a school corridor after a Christmas play, flowers and a green-faced ten year old, the ordinary geometry of a life in tact. She felt the woman's smile land on her like a question she hadn't been asked and didn't know how to answer. She smiled back. It was the smile she had become skilled at, the one that confirmed what people needed to see without committing to anything.

They ended up at Mitch's house. This was how Saturday evenings went now.

Emily dropped her backpack and the flowers and the Grinch hat in a single pile and went immediately to the living room.

Mitch had recently bought a television that occupied most of one wall, and Emily had opinions about this that she expressed primarily through proximity. She sat cross-legged on the rug in front of it.

"What do you want?" Mitch asked from the kitchen. "I've got the pasta thing you liked."

"Yes please," Emily called, not looking up.

Paige stood in the space between the kitchen and the living room, jacket still on.

She watched Emily on the rug.

The Grinch hat was still in the pile by the door. Through the kitchen doorway she could hear Mitch opening and closing cupboards, the soft percussion of a meal being prepared. Music from the television.

Paige stood there and she let herself see it clearly.

This was what she had been not seeing for months, or seeing peripherally, in the defocused way you look at things that are too close to examine directly. The ease of it. The quality of the ease. Emily on the rug as though the rug was hers. Mitch in the kitchen as though the kitchen were shared. Herself standing in the space between them, jacket still on, still technically a visitor in a life that had been quietly organizing itself around her.

She sat on the couch.

She thought about the woman in the corridor and her smile.

She thought about what it would mean to let that smile be accurate.

She took her jacket off.

Emily glanced back.

"You were really good tonight," Paige said.

"I know," said Emily, the same way she said it to Mitch, but softer this time. More private.

She paused and looked at her mom. "Mrs. Okafor

said I could be in the spring show too. The older kids one."

"Do you want to be?"

Emily considered. "Maybe."

She added, "Dad would have liked the Grinch."

Paige kept her face very still.

"He would have," she said.

He would have loved the Grinch.

That part stayed simple.

He would have laughed too loud. Emily would have loved it and pretended not to. She knew that. Some things didn't change. They stayed where you left them.

She let her eyes move through the room.

The television. The warmth. Mitch in the kitchen, opening cupboards, not asking anything. Emily on the rug like she belonged there. Like she always had.

She felt how much she wanted that.

She sat with the wanting and she did not look away from it. She had been looking away from it for months, managing it the way she managed everything, filling it under things that required more examination than she currently had the capacity for, things she would return to when the immediate pressures were handled and the second column was shorter and Emily settled. The second column was never going to be shorter. Emily was never going to be fully settled in the way that released Paige from the responsibility of settling her. She understood that now. The examination she had been postponing was going to find a more convenient moment. This was the moment. Mitch in the kitchen and Emily on the rug and herself on the couch with her jacket off.

She let herself look directly at it.

She wanted this. The three bowls. The sound of the kitchen. Emily on the rug, knees pulled in, like it was hers. She wanted it with a force that surprised her. It was large and it was real and it had been building across two years of Mitch showing up without agenda and Emily moving her chess pieces from one shelf to another.

She didn't trust how much she wanted it.

It wasn't because wanting it was wrong. She had released herself from the idea that wanting it was wrong approximately three months ago. In a conversation with her mother who said, you are allowed to want a life, Paige. She had hung up with it and sat with it and eventually believed it.

She was tired. It wasn't the kind that passed. Mitch had made things lighter. She did not know if she could fully trust a wanting that had been born in exhaustion. She did not know if the ease that she felt was love or relief or the simple animal comfort of not being alone, and she was not certain those things were as different as she once believed.

Jake had not chosen to leave Emily.

She still believed that.

She believed it, like a bond you keep intact because breaking it would change too much at once.

But he was gone.

And she was here.

And this was here.

She didn't try to put those things into something that made sense.

She kept her eyes on Emily.

The guilt came with it.

She let it stay.

It didn't cancel anything. It didn't explain anything either. It sat there with everything else.

Later when Mitch had brought out two bowls and a smaller one for Emily on the coffee table, when the three of them sat in the warm noise of television and Emily had worked her way through most of her pasta and was starting to lose the fight against tiredness, Paige said it quietly.

"Em. How would you feel about spending more time here?"

Emily's spoon moved through what was left of her pasta.

"Like sleepovers?" she said.

"Like more than that. Like being here more regularly."

Emily looked at the television. A cartoon bird was attempting to fly upside down and failing cheerfully.

"Would my stuff be here?" she asked.

"My books?"

"Whatever you wanted."

Emily's spoon stopped moving.

Paige waited.

"Okay," Emily said.

Paige looked at her. The straight back. The chin on her knees.

"You can say if it's not okay," Paige said. "You can always say."

Emily nodded.

The television filled the space between them.

Paige stayed where she was. The small nod settled, heavier than it looked.

She didn't try to name it.

She knew better than that.

And Paige sat in the warm light of Mitch's living room with the weight of that small nod in her chest.

She didn't move.

Chapter Thirty-Two

Jake notices the park when winter breaks. The ache in his knee before rain. The quiet reshuffling of who sleeps where and who doesn't come back at all.

He learns where to be when the city cleans itself and where not to be when it doesn't. He learns which churches lock their doors early, which kitchens don't ask questions, which corners look safe and which ones only look that way.

The cart changes. So do the blankets. The jacket from last winter lasts two more, then doesn't.

One stretch of winter comes harder than the rest.

The cold came without snow at first, kept dropping after dark until it was something else entirely. By evening even men who brag about making it through anything, are quieter. Their hands stay buried in their pockets. Nobody lingers unless they have to.

Jake lasts as long as he can.

He walks to stay warm. Circles blocks, he knows. Slips into subway stations long enough to feel heat on his face before someone tells him to move. By midnight his knee is stiff, fingers hurt, and the cold has made its way through every layer he has.

A few days earlier, someone said two men were found frozen behind a loading dock uptown. Jake keeps walking. Then he doesn't.

The department store is dark except for the security lights and the glow of the display window at street level. Around the side of the building, half-hidden from the road, is an emergency exit stairwell he has noticed before and never tried. He presses the metal bar.

Unlocked.

Heat meets him immediately. Not warm. Not freezing. Jake steps inside and lets the door close behind him. The stairwell smells faintly of concrete dust and industrial cleaner. The railing was grey, the steps grey, something humming faintly somewhere in the walls. He sits first.

Then, when nothing happens, he lowers himself onto the landing between floors and pulls his coat around him. His cart stays wedged beside the door downstairs, half-hidden from view. He listens for footsteps, for voices, for the crackle of a radio. Nothing. His body starts shaking once the cold begins to leave it. Harder than before. He presses his hands under his arms and closes his eyes.

For an hour. Until he can feel his feet again.

He wakes up to a flashlight on his face. Jake jerks too fast, pain cutting through his knee.

A security guard stands two steps above him. Around Jake's age. Maybe younger. Dark jacket, badge clipped crooked, radio at his shoulder. He looks tired more than dangerous.

"You can't be here," the guard says.

Jake blinks against the light. "I know."

"You need to leave."

Jake gets one hand on the rail and tries to stand. The warmth has made the outside feel farther away.

"It's really cold," he says.

The guard says nothing.

Jake looks toward the door at the bottom of the stairs, then back at him.

"I don't think I make it out there tonight."

The guard shifts his weight.

"There's shelters."

Jake shakes his head once. "No."

The guard frowns. "Why not."

Jake grips the railing harder.

"Not doing shelters."

The answer hangs there. The guard glances toward the door above them, then down the stairwell, then back at Jake. He looks like he might radio someone, or call it in. Instead, he rubs a hand over his mouth and lets out a long breath.

"Okay," he says. "Just tonight."

Jake doesn't move.

The guard looks at him. "You hear me?"

Jake nods.

"You stay right here. You don't wander. You don't leave a mess. And you're gone before morning staff comes in."

"Okay."

"I can get fired for this."

"I know."

The guard reaches past him, clicks off the flashlight, and the stairwell goes dim again.

"Thank you," Jake says.

The guard is heading back up.

"Yeah," he says, not turning around. "Be gone early."

The door closes behind him. Jake stays sitting for a

long time after that. He doesn't move. Eventually he curls against the wall and sleeps in pieces. When he wakes, the stairwell is still dim and silent. He leaves the landing exactly as he found it. Outside, the cold is still there waiting.

By the time the weather begins to turn, the rain comes sideways for three days straight. Jake pushes the cart into the tree line at the edge of the park and stops.

He has a tarp. Blue. Torn at one corner. Scavenged from a construction site weeks earlier. He has rope and four bungee cords and an instinct he doesn't remember learning.

He works. Rope between two oaks. Tarp folded over the line. Corners pulled tight and anchored to roots. The tear he patches with duct tape from the cart. It takes twenty minutes. It holds. He crawls underneath and pulls the cart beside him. Rain hits the tarp in hard scattered drops. Then steady. Then constant. Rain on plastic and the smell of wet earth. Jake lies on his back and listens. His chest tightens unexpectedly. A thin rivulet of water begins threading its way along the ground toward him. He shifts two inches left. The rain keeps going.

By the middle of summer, the park fills again. One morning a race, cuts straight through it. Jake hears it before he sees it, the distant static PA system, an announcers voice carried and broken by wind, and then the sound of hundreds of feet moving together. Soft and collective. Jake pushes the cart off the main path and onto the grass.

The lead runners come first. Four of them. Spread

across the width of the path. Faces blank with focus.

They pass without seeing anything that isn't the next stretch of pavement. Then the field arrives.

Wave after wave, charity shirts, watches flashing in the sun. Some grimacing. Some laughing with the person beside them.

A volunteer station further down the path. Paper cups stacked in towers, two teenagers shouting encouragement to anyone who will hear it. Jake watches from the grass.

Then one runner slows slightly. He didn't stop but eased off slightly. He studies Jake longer than necessary. He keeps running.

Jake stands there until the last runners pass. Until the sound of their footsteps fades completely. Only then does he move again.

When the leaves begin turning and the air sharpens again, a reporter arrives in the camp.

She was young, holding a recorder, a tote bag from some local paper slung over one shoulder. Ray watches her approach.

"Here it comes," he says.

She interviews Terrence first. Hands moving. Recorder held up. She notices Jake. Ray nudges him.

"Another face for the story."

Jake lifts the cart handles. She stops near him.

"I'm asking people what this place means to them."

Jake looks at the recorder. At the press badge around her neck. He imagines the article. "I'm good," he says.

She nods. Doesn't push. Moves on.

Ray watches her leave. "No words for the lady."

"I know."

"What's the difference."

Jake looks around the camp. At the tents. At the trees. At Terrence still speaking into the recorder.

"He's telling his story," Jake says.

"I'm still in mine."

Three weeks later the city arrives with trucks.

They come early, before the light has fully settled. Two sanitation vehicles and a white van Jake didn't recognize were parked along the path. Men in vests moved through the camp with clipboards. Tents coming down and belongings separated into piles. A police cruiser idling at the far end of the path.

Ray was gone before they came. Jake had his cart handles-up when the van door opened.

Three people stepped out. They were not city workers. They wore different vests carrying backpacks and a plastic crate with supplies. Jake recognized them from other clearings. They were part of the street medicine outreach program. A woman with a clipboard was scanning faces as she walked. She stopped when she reached Jake.

"Jake," she said.

He looked at her.

"I've got you on our list from the Millward intake. A while back now." She opened the clipboard, ran a finger down a column. "You were flagged for a standing prescription. Extended release for the knee."

She said the name of it. He hadn't heard it spoken aloud in a long time.

"We've got a community health contact who can

authorize a refill. It's not a complicated ask." She said, "I need a yes from you and we do the rest."

Around them the camp was coming down. Somone argued near the tree line. A tent pole fell onto the path.

Jake's eyes moved to his cart, the bag where he kept things. He looked back at her.

"No," he said.

She waited, in case there was more.

She raised her pen and drew a line through a document on the clipboard. "Okay," she said. "We've got ibuprofen and basic wound care if you need it."

"I'm alright."

She nodded. Moved to the man beside Jake's cart without pressing further.

Jake lifted the handles and pushed the cart east. He didn't look back at the camp.

People begin to recognize him. He didn't know most of their names. They didn't know his. He watches bags when someone steps away. He gives directions without expecting anything back, breaks food in half without thinking. When a new guy shows up shaking and too proud to ask, Jake leaves an apple where it can be found.

Some mornings he hears runners before dawn and doesn't look. Other days he watches. He can tell who's new to it. Who runs angry. Who's only running.

And then one morning, behind the Midtown Fitness Centre, Jake pauses beside a torn garbage bag. Morning light hadn't reached the alley yet. The air is still blue-grey with early cold. He crouches carefully because of the knee and brushes aside a strip of plastic.

A pair of running shoes. They were used, but the soles hadn't given up yet. The mesh was dusty, but the laces were still thick and heavy in his hands.

He stares at them but doesn't touch them at first.

He lifts them by the heels. The soles hold faint imprint of miles run by someone else. Jake sets them on the dumpster lid.

He stops without deciding to.

Lifts the shoes again.

Tucks them carefully into the canvas bag on his cart.

He doesn't put them on. Not yet.

He pushes the cart out of the alley.

Chapter Thirty-Three

He smelled it before he saw it. Woodsmoke threading through cold air, and underneath it a scent faintly metallic from the barrel heating up. Then voices. More than he expected. A group that had been long enough to be comfortable, laughter arriving in short bursts, conversations, people sharing an evening together.

Then... a harmonica.

Quiet. Off to the side.

The fire was set in a clearing off the tree line, far enough from the path to be ignored by the city. A steel barrel at the center, flames pulling upward in the cold. Folding chairs arranged in a loose circle, mismatched, sourced from different decades and different lives. Milk crates, an overturned bucket that someone was sitting on.

Maybe fourteen people. Men mostly. Different ages, different wear on their faces.

At the edge of the firelight, slightly apart from the main circle sat the man with the harmonica.

He was older, or looked it. He wore a dark wig that sat slightly off, like it had been put on without a mirror and left that way, the hair catching the firelight one side and disappearing into the shadow on the other. He held the harmonica loosely in one hand, playing with his eyes closed, somewhere between here and wherever the music took him.

Jake noticed him. Noticed the wig and then glanced at Ray.

Ray was looking at the fire.

Jake noticed. The harmonica continued, quiet and rhythmic. Nobody reacted. The music was expected and the wig was his.

Ray walked into the clearing without announcing himself. Two people acknowledged him immediately. A nod from a heavyset man near the barrel and a hand raised from across the fire by a woman Jake hadn't fully seen yet.

"Ray." Someone said.

"Who's the friend?" someone else asked.

Ray didn't look back at Jake.

"This is Jake," he said.

The man running the event was impossible to miss.

He stood slightly apart from the folding chairs near a wooden cable spool that had been repurposed as a table. White hair, greased back. Jeans rolled once at the bottom with a small black comb visible in his back pocket.

He was counting bills from a coffee tin, doing it with attention, doing it with ceremony, pressing each one flat against his palm before adding it to the stack.

"Smitty," Ray said, when the count finished.

Smitty looked up. He assessed Jake with the unhurried attention of a man who had been assessing people for a long time. His eyes went to Jake's arms first then his face.

"Player?" he said.

"Just watching," Ray said.

Smitty looked at Jake's arms again with the expression of a man confirming a suspicion.

"Five dollars entry," he said. "You decide to stop just

watching."

He tucked the bills into his shirt pocket and turned back to the cable spool without waiting for an answer.

Across the fire the harmonica's tempo shifted.

The tournament had its own logic explained to Jake in fragments by Ray.

Five dollars to enter. Winner takes the pot minus what Smitty called operating costs. Matches were decided by best of three. No time limit. No weight class.

"Is it rigged?" Jake asked.

Ray considered.

"It's Smitty's," he said.

The first match was set up. Two men at the cable spool, elbows down, hands locked waiting. Smitty crouched slightly. He looked at neither of them. He focused at a point in the middle distance.

Then, he said.

"Fonzie."

They went.

Jake glanced at Ray.

Jake looked back. The larger man was winning, Then, he wasn't. The smaller man had something technical happening in his wrist, some leverage that changed the geometry of the grip, and after forty-five seconds the larger man's knuckles touched the spool and Smitty said "there it is".

The small man raised one fist. Nobody cheered but the result was noted.

Smitty paid out from the coffee tin.

Behind it all Cecil played on, quiet and continuous.

"What does that mean?" Jake said to Ray. "Fonzie."

From across the fire, without looking up, without any indication she had been listening, a woman's voice arrived sharp and dry and finished the question before Jake had fully asked it.

"Honey. Don't ask."

Her name, Ray told him, was Rhonda.

She was sitting on a folding chair at the far edge of the fire circle with the posture of someone who hadn't always sat in folding chairs.

She wore a coat that had been good once and still carried the memory of it in the cut of the shoulders. Her hair was wrapped, silver at the temples.

New York was still in her. You could hear it.

She was looking at Jake with a calm assessment.

"You're the runner," she said.

Jake looked at Ray.

Ray shrugged.

"Ray talks," Rhonda said. "Don't flatter yourself, he talks about everyone."

She crossed her legs.

"You got a girlfriend?"

Jake blinked. "No."

"Boyfriend?"

"No."

"Hm." She studied him a moment longer. "Shame. You've got good bone structure. It's being wasted."

From somewhere to Jake's left a man made a sound that was half laugh half cough.

Someone else said "here she goes."

The group had the settled quality of an audience that knew this performance well.

"I'm fine," Jake said.

"You're cold and you're skinny," Rhonda said. "That's not fine." She tilted her head. "You always this talkative or is tonight special?"

He's warming up," Ray said.

"He better. It's very cold right now."

More laughter from the circle. Jake felt the warmth of being, the target of people who didn't mean anything by it.

Across the fire Cecil looked up from his harmonica directly at Jake. A steady unhurried look of a man who had seen people arrive at this fire in every possible condition and had learned to read what they were carrying.

He held Jakes's eyes.

He brought the harmonica back to his mouth and played.

That was Cecil's greeting.

Smitty ran three more bouts with the same ceremony. The same crouching,

"Fonzie."

Each time. Flat and practiced.

Between matches he stood near the cable spool and accepted or declined conversation at his own discretion. Someone asked him a question about seeding the next bout like it mattered. He ran a hand back over his hair once and the comb went back into the pocket with the same smooth motion.

"How long's he been doing this?" Jake asked Ray.

Ray thought about it. "Long as I've been her," he said. "Longer probably."

Rhonda heard this across the fire and didn't look up from whatever she was considering.

"Smitty's been saying that since before you were lost, honey," she said.

She said it lightly.

The fire shifted. Jake looked at it.

Cecil played a slower tune.

The second bout produced the evening's best result, a man nobody had bet on, winning three straight, in under two minutes, each one faster than the last. He didn't celebrate. He leaned back and accepted what Smitty counted out.

The third bout went the other way. Long back and forth. Smitty watched it with attention, arms folded. When it finally ended, he paid out, made a notation on a folded piece of paper and looked around the circle.

His eyes landed on Jake.

"You sure?" he said.

"About what," Jake said.

Smitty studied at his arms again. "Five dollars. Easy money tonight."

"Leave him alone, Smitty," Rhonda said, without looking up.

Smitty looked at her. "I'm offering an opportunity."

"You're offering entertainment. It's not the same thing,"

He looked at Jake.

"Open offer," he said, and returned to the cable spool.

From behind someone laughed. Smitty did not acknowledge this. He ran a hand over his hair, checked the comb, slipped it back.

Cecil played on.

Smitty watched Jake from across the fire. "How old are you."

Jake told him.

Smitty nodded once, like he was confirming a feeling he'd calculated. "My daughter's probably your age." He didn't say it to anyone in particular. He turned back to the cable spool.

The music shifted somewhere around the fourth bout.

A change in what Cecil was playing, something with more rhythm to it, and a pulse.

Cecil's eyes were closed now, the harmonica in both hands, playing with the concentration of a man alone in a room. The wig caught the firelight on one side. His foot moving slightly against the ground, just feeling it.

Rhonda stood up.

The group noticed this, how groups notice when someone who tends to do something is about to do it.

"No," said the man next to Jake, grinning.

"Absolutely not," said someone else with great feeling.

"Oh yes,' said Rhonda, to no one in particular.

She looked across the fire at jake.

Jake became aware of this looking.

"No," he said.

"He speaks," Rhonda said. "In complete sentences even."

"I don't dance."

"Everybody dances."

"I really don't."

"Honey." She deployed the word with the patience of a woman who had heard every available version of no and treated them all as temporary.

"I am from New York City. I have been dancing since before this park existed. I danced on stages that would make your eyes water. I have performed for audiences that are now dead in the natural way." She paused to let this land. "I am asking you for one song around a barrel fire. What exactly is your objection."

The group had gathered opinions about this. They were expressed simultaneously and at volume. Someone said Jake's name in a tone that contained an entire argument. Someone else spoke in another language that produced significant laughter from three people who understood it.

Ray said nothing.

He was looking at the fire.

But there was an expression at the corner of his mouth that had not been there before.

Cecil opened his eyes briefly, looked at Rhonda, and shifted into a melody with slightly more rhythm without being asked. He was aware what was happening. He'd seen it before. The music changed to accommodate what the evening was becoming.

Jake stood up.

The sound from the group suggested this was the correct and overdue decision.

He was terrible.

His arms didn't know what to do with themselves. His feet spent years moving in straight lines at measured paces but he had no existing framework for this. He was aware of every person watching him and that awareness made everything worse.

Rhonda was not terrible.

She took his hand and did something with her posture that changed the situation. She had been a dancer in a different life, in a different city, on stages that existed now only in the memory of people who had been there, and that life was gone but the body remembered every bit of it with perfect fidelity.

For a few seconds she stopped playing to the crowd and moved. Her posture changed. She wasn't there.

It lasted maybe four seconds.

Jake saw it.

Neither of them said anything,

Then she looked down at his footwork and made a face of genuine suffering.

"You run for a living and this is what you do with your feet?"

The group reacted with laughter.

"Former," Jake said.

"Former runner or former feet?"

The man on the milk crate lost his footing entirely. Someone caught him. This produced its own wave of noise.

Jake laughed.

Rhonda nodded once.

Cecil played them to the end of it, the harmonica continuing after Rhonda let go of Jake's hand.

Rhonda sat back in her folding chair with the full composure of a woman who had known exactly how this was going to go from the moment she stood up.

"New York," she said to no one in particular. Smoothing her coat. "We don't produce bad dancers."

The last bout was a long one.

Smitty crouched.

His eyes went to the middle distance.

"Fonzie."

The smaller man lost.

Smitty paid out.

He looked around the circle one more time with the expression of a man closing his event with satisfaction.

His eyes landed on Jake.

"No footwork," he said. Not unkindly. "Work on it."

He walked away before Jake could respond.

Ray watched him go. "He means it as a compliment," he said.

"How can you tell"

"He talked to you."

People began drifting. The natural dispersal of a group whose shared purpose had concluded. Conversations broke into smaller one and then into none.

Rhonda stood, adjusted her coat and looked at Jake one last time.

"You should eat more," she said. "I like my men with a little muscle."

"I'll work on it," Jake said.

"See that you do."

She turned to go and paused behind Cecil, who was sitting with the dying fire, harmonica resting in his open palm. She placed one hand briefly on his shoulder without stopping, without saying anything. He didn't look up. He was looking at the fire with the quiet attention of a man who had enjoyed seeing it go out.

She was gone before he finished looking.

Cecil sat a moment longer. Then he tucked the harmonica into his breast pocket. He stood, adjusted his wig with two fingers, made a small private gesture and walked off into the dark.

Jake watched him go.

"What's his story?" Jake asked.

Ray looked at where Cecil had been.

"Cecil's story is Cecil's," he said.

Jake nodded

Fair enough.

Ray sat beside him on the overturned bucket, both of them looking at what remained of the fire. The barrel ticked as the metal cooled.

"She was good," Jake said. "Rhonda. When she was really dancing. Those few seconds "

"Yeah," Ray said.

"Has she always been like that? Here I mean."

Ray thought about it. "Rhonda's been to a lot of places," he said. "This is the current one."

Jake looked at the fire.

Smitty passed behind them on his way out, coffee tin under one arm, patting his air once with his free hand. He glanced at Jake without stopping.

"Five dollars next time," he said. "Think about it.'

He walked into the dark. The grease in his hair caught the last firelight and he was gone, just the sound of his footsteps.

Ray stood.

"You did alright tonight," he said.

Ray walked toward his corner of the park.

Jake stayed by the dying fire a while longer.

His hands rested on his knees. He became aware after a while that he was tapping one foot very slightly against the ground. It wasn't a runner's rhythm, something slower. A beat from the harmonica. From those few seconds when Rhonda had stopped performing and danced.

He stopped when he noticed it, then let it continue.

Chapter Thirty-Four

Footsteps passed. Shoes scuffed pavement. Somewhere nearby, a leash jingled.

He looked up.

A whippet moved slowly along the path, her steps measured now, gray dusting her muzzle. A young woman walked beside her, speaking into her phone.

Jake froze.

The dog paused.

Sniffed the air.

Her head tilted slightly, listening.

"Come on, Dolce," the woman said, pulling on the leash.

Dolce.

The name brushed a feeling inside him.

He saw it.

The heart shape.

It was her.

He smiled before he meant to.

The smile that came was small and real and surprised.

The woman and the dog moved on, the leash slack between them. Dolce didn't hurry. She didn't strain to keep up. She walked, steady and calm, like time had finally stopped asking her to be fast.

He watched them until they disappeared around the curve. He didn't move after that. Sitting felt right and that bench was there and the park kept doing what parks do.

A father jogged past with a stroller, one hand on the handle, the other holding a phone he wasn't looking at. A woman in a red coat walked, head down, eating a wrap from a paper bag. Two kids on bikes cut across the grass and one of them shouted chicken at the other that made them both laugh.

Jake watched all of it.

Years of being invisible had changed how he saw things.

The woman in red didn't know. Nobody did.

Dolce had looked at him.

That was all.

A dog pausing on a path, head tilted, recognizing a presence in the air that the woman beside her didn't think to look for.

He exhaled.

His hand moved before he decided to, reaching toward the canvas bag strapped to the cart. His fingers found the laces first. Then the mesh. He pulled the shoes out and set them on the ground in front of him.

They were not his shoes. They never had been. They belonged to someone who had run miles in them, whose feet had shaped the soles, who had set them down one day without understanding they were being left behind. Jake understood that now in a way he hadn't when he lifted them from the dumpster lid. He had carried them for weeks.

He was ready now.

He leaned forward and slipped one foot in, then the other. The fit was close enough. He tugged the laces tight like he always had, two fingers hooked through the loop, pulling until the shoe sat against his foot.

He sat back.

He stood and took a step. Then another.

The shoes made a different step against the path than his boots had. Softer and closer to the ground. He had forgotten that, how running shoes changed the texture of the world underfoot.

He walked.

He wasn't walking anywhere specific but walked forward. He didn't know where he was going but for the first time in a long time, he didn't feel like standing still. He didn't rush. Jake walked. The path curved ahead, gentle and familiar. His footfalls sounded different in these shoes. Lighter than everything else he wore.

He felt it in his shoulders as they relaxed, his breathing settling into a rhythm.

A jogger drifted past him, earbuds in, oblivious. Years ago, he would have measured. Converted numbers into potential. Now he didn't. He watched the motion and let it pass. He walked a little farther than he meant to. The bench he'd started from was well behind him now. He noticed the pond. The cold ripple on the water. Ducks carving lazy paths across the surface. A kid on a scooter, laughing too loudly.

His knee ached but it was an honest ache.

He stopped and he stood there, hands in his pockets,

looking at the path ahead, then back at the distance he'd covered. It wasn't far.

He sat on a nearby bench, slower this time, careful not to jar the joint. He leaned forward, elbows on his knees, staring at the shoes.

He brushed his thumb across the fabric.

A breeze moved through the trees. Leaves rustled. Somewhere behind him a dog barked and a woman laughed.

He sat like that, not thinking forward, or back, staying where he was. When the light began to tilt toward evening and shadows stretched out across the path, Jake stood again. He adjusted the strap on his cart and he walked.

And somewhere, half a park away, the memory of a dog named Dolce trotted calmly along with him, not sprinting, moving at a pace that life could live with.

Chapter Thirty-Five

At first, Jake pretends he isn't doing anything different.

He tells himself he's walking a little more because the days are getting lighter. Because the park feels easier to stay in when the sun doesn't hide.

He takes a second lap one morning. Then a third another day. He doesn't measure distance in strides anymore. In how long he can stay inside his own body before it reminds him why he stopped trusting it.

Some days the knee aches right away, a familiar warning. Some days it flares halfway through and he stops, stretches, waits, then limps the rest, resigned but not surprised. And then there are the other days, the days where it doesn't hurt.

Those days feel wrong. It starts small, an easy step, a good placement. Hips shift and shoulders loosen and breath falls into rhythm without being asked.

And then, before he can talk himself out of it, he jogs.

Ten meters. Maybe fifteen. A handful of seconds.

He stops after each attempt and checks to see if anyone saw.

He looks around.

Nobody cares. He tells himself good. He wouldn't want witnesses anyway. He tries again another day. Tiny bursts. A few strides. A slow return to walking like nothing happened.

And sometimes the pain comes late and bites him hard, and he nods. But sometimes, sometimes it doesn't bite at all.

Those days feel wrong. If it doesn't hurt, then it wasn't the knee. You could've kept going. So what was the rest of it.

He hates that voice. He hates how familiar it sounds. He hates how much of it is his own. By night, the city cools and the park thins. People go somewhere. He doesn't. He lies down with the others tucked into shadows and corners and hollow spaces. He makes himself smaller. He shifts the blanket. He curls around the ache in his leg.

He waits for the pain to roar. It doesn't. It pulses. His throat tightens. He pulls the blanket over his face so no one sees. He presses his jaw shut to keep whatever's inside from getting out. It doesn't work.

Tears come slow.

Then harder.

Chapter Thirty-Six

The cab from the airport took forty minutes because of construction.

He paid the driver and carried his own bags to the door.

Inside, the house had the fullness he still wasn't entirely used to. Emily's backpack hanging on the hook by the door. Paige's cardigan folded over the arm of the chair in that way she had. He set his bag down and stood in it.

He went down the hall.

The trophy room had been his father's idea in concept.

The shelving and the lighting. How things were arranged, by feel, that made sense to someone who understood what each thing had cost.

He wasn't sure why he came in now.

He clicked the light on.

The room settled into its familiar arrangement around him. Shelves along three walls. The trophies from high school on the lower left. Above them the collegiate ones. The framed photographs. The team shots. The regional and national championship plaques his father had insisted on mounting rather than leaving in boxes. And the medals. Hung on small hooks along the back wall, arranged by year.

He found the right hook for the bronze.

He hung it carefully.

Stepped back.

It sat between the silver from the indoor nationals three years ago and a gap where the gold would have gone, where he had always privately imagined the gold would go. He looked at the gap without expression. Then he looked at the bronze. It was a good medal. He had run the race he was capable of. He ran on that day against those men under those conditions and this was the result. There was no version of athletic life that required an apology. His father's voice would find the gap before it found the medal.

He turned slightly, not looking for anything in particular.

And he saw it.

The clipping was in the upper right corner, mounted in a simple frame, slightly off center. He had put it here himself, years ago, early in his collegiate career when the idea of being written about in those terms still felt like worth marking. He couldn't remember the last time he had actually looked at it.

He looked at it now.

Two figures mid-stride on a track, the image caught at the angle that flattened depth and made both runners look like they were occupying the same plane of motion.

Two Springfield Runners Competing for National Limelight

His name was in the first paragraph, his times, his trajectory, the whole inevitable arc of it. Jake's name was in the second paragraph.

Mitch read it. He hadn't done that in a long time. The writer had been generous. He noted the late start, the walk-on status. There was a quote from Roberts revealing how he felt about both of them.

Mitch stood in front of the clipping and read Jake's name and thought about the last time he had seen him.

Then a memory arrived. All at once.

A corridor at the national championships. The indoor meet, five years after Springfield. Mitch was walking from the warm-up area to the call room, still in his training jacket, headphones around his neck, focused in the way that closed everything down to breath and cadence and the race he had been running in his head since Wednesday.

A runner fell into step beside him briefly. Tall, loose-limbed, from a program out west. They had met at a couple of meets before, the easy familiarity of athletes who competed in the same circuit without ever being rivals. The man talked about the heat in the building, about the schedule running long. Mitch half-listened, nodding.

Then the man said, "whatever happened to that guy on your team? Clark? Jake?"

Mitch stopped walking.

The corridor kept moving around him. Officials with clipboards. Runners in spikes, headphones, the focused blankness of people preparing to compete.

"Hear his life is really messed up." the man said. He

wasn't being cruel. He was making conversation like athletes do in corridors.

"Someone said he's been living rough. Like actually on the streets. You believe that? Guy like that ends up." He shook his head. A sound that was almost a laugh but wasn't. The sound people make, when something is so outside their understanding to process seriously.

Mitch heard the words. "Where?" he asked.

The man shrugged. "In Springfield, I think. Someone from your school mentioned it. Said they'd seen him."

He glanced at Mitch. "You didn't know?"

Mitch thought about the flight home that evening. About Emily asleep when he landed. About Paige leaving the kitchen light on the way she always did when he came in later.

"No," Mitch said.

The man nodded, moving on. "Crazy how things go," he said, and walked ahead toward the call room.

Mitch stood in the corridor.

Around him the meet continued. Voices. Footsteps. The crackle of a PA system calling names. Somewhere ahead the gun would fire and people would run and times would be recorded.

He stood there. He put his headphones on. And he walked to the call room.

That night he had come home to Paige. Emily had been nine or ten, asleep, the small silence of a house with a sleeping child in it. Paige was in the kitchen, her hair down, the comfortable version of herself that she only allowed in private. She had asked about the race. He told her. She made tea and they had sat at the kitchen table and talked about the weekend and what Emily had done and a joke Emily's teacher had made at pickup that Paige had been saving to tell him.

Mitch sat at that table and said nothing. Not that night nor the next morning. Nor in the weeks that followed, when the information settled into him.

He had told himself it was unconfirmed. That corridor gossip at a meet was not a source. That the right thing to do was verify before saying anything that would upset Paige or raise a question that neither of them knew how to answer.

He had not verified. He had told himself there was nothing to be done. That Jake had made his choices. That people ended in difficult situations because of decisions they had made and not made and that inserting himself into someone else's consequences was presumptuous at best and destructive at worst.

He had believed some of that. Not all of it.

He had told himself finally, in the version of the story he had been living inside for years, that saying something would have broken what they had built. That Paige would have felt responsible. That Emily would have been confused and hurt in ways she was too young to carry. That he was protecting the people he loved by absorbing this thing quietly and alone. He had believed that too.

He was still not sure how much of it was true.

Now, he stood in the warm light of the trophy room with the bronze medal on its hook and Jake's name in faded newsprint. There had been a version of that headline that ended differently for both of them, and he had been the one it ended well for, and he had done nothing wrong, and he had also done nothing.

He was still looking at the clipping when he heard it.

The front door.

Emily's voice first, high and bright, mid-sentence about her day at school. Then the lower register of Paige's response, patient, almost laughing. The sound of shoes dropped by the door.

Mitch looked at the clipping for one more moment. He reached up and straightened the frame. He turned the light off. Closed the door.

Chapter Thirty-Seven

Late afternoon in the park.

The park had that tired quiet to it, when the heat leaks out of the day and people start breathing easier. Jake walked the path slow, steady.

Ahead of him, two joggers had stopped near the water fountain, mid-thirties, flushed and grinning, shaking out their arms. One guzzled water. The other leaned on the railing, stretching, talking about splits and how the last kilometer "killed him."

Jake kept walking. He didn't want to look.

The man stretching glanced over. Paused and looked again. Recognition came slowly. It built. He squinted, trying to place him.

"Hold on," he said. "No way…"

Jake kept walking.

The guy took a small step forward.

"Hey, sorry," he said, breathless still. "This is going to sound crazy but… are you, Jake?"

Jake's steps hesitated before stopping. He turned slightly. The man studied him harder, then the disbelief turned into a grin of certainty.

"You are. You're Jake. Springfield Jake."

Identity, spoken aloud after years. Jake didn't answer.

The second jogger wandered closer, curious now.

"Who's…" "This guy," the first one said, pointing towards Jake. "He was a monster back in college track. You remember those clips? Conference finals? That closing kick out of nowhere?”

The second man blinked, then his face opened with late recognition. “Ohhhhh… him.” He looked at Jake with respect. There was no pity.

“Man,” the first runner said, shaking his head with an amazed kind of nostalgia. “You used to fly. My old coach made us study your form. Said you were what ‘efficient’ looked like.”

Jake shifted, realizing they weren’t mocking him.

The first jogger wiped sweat from his forehead and laughed.

“Crazy timing, too. You hear about the big charity race they’re hyping up?”

Jake blinked. “No.”

“Yeah,” the guy said, excited again. “They’re bringing back Mitch. Headlining it. Big hometown return story. Posters going up everywhere. Media’s eating it up. Olympian comes back to where it all started.”

Mitch. The name hit him.

The jogger didn’t notice the impact.

“City’s making a big deal out of it. Guess they want people to remember what the old days felt like. Those two…” he stopped himself, grinning. “Man, those races? You and him? Best stuff I ever saw.”

The guy finally seemed to realize this might be… personal. He softened.

“Anyway. Didn’t mean to weird you out. But… had to say. You were special to watch.”

The second jogger nodded. “Legend,” he said.

They didn’t linger. A nod and a quiet goodbye. They jogged off, leaving Jake standing alone.

Chapter Thirty-Eight

He ran. It wasn't far at first, but with the stubbornness of someone who stopped asking for permission from his own body. The knee held in that reluctant way it had recently.

The park path connected to the trail system the way it always had, the network of linked routes that threaded through the city's green spaces and out toward the quieter neighborhoods beyond. He had run sections of it years ago in another life, logging miles in the early morning before the city was fully awake. That version of him didn't follow him here.

He ran without checking his pace or watching others.

The park gave way to a bike path that ran south along the river. The path was familiar. His stride used to open here. Now it negotiated. The university district fell away behind him. Then the commercial strips. Then the older neighborhoods where the townhouses sit further back from the road and the trees were taller. He didn't notice any of it consciously. His feet were making decisions his mind hadn't been consulted on.

The trail narrowed into wood boards, hollow underfoot. Then crossed a footbridge he didn't consciously recognize but whose board sounded good under his feet. The city thinned around him gradually, the density of building softening into older streets, lower roofline, more sky. He wasn't tracking distance. His eyes were on the path immediately ahead and his breathing took over before his thoughts could catch up.

He ran through intersections where the trail dipped under roads. At some point the trail crossed under the highway on a concrete path that smelled of damp and exhaust and came out the other side into something quieter.

The buildings stopped. The valley floor opened up south of the city, wide and flat, Coast Range sitting low to the west, the Cascades further east, both ranges always present in the valley. The sky was the grey-white of an Oregon morning. He had been running long enough that his breathing had found its own rhythm.

He ran past soccer fields, past dog walkers, past a water fountain he stopped at briefly without registering where he was. He passed a green highway marker without reading it. A mile further a grain elevator rose from the flat ground on his left, white-painted, the name of a cooperative stenciled in faded letters near the top. He had seen the elevator before. From the seat of a car. From a bus window but he didn't make the connection.

At some point, the surrounding began to change in a way that reached him slowly. The path had moved and the light came through differently here, softer than the open valley light. The width of the path. The curve. A stone retaining wall along the eastern edge. His eyes went to it without thinking.

He slowed without deciding to and his stride shortened. His breathing changed. The trail opened ahead of him into the wide path that ran alongside the soccer field, a familiar narrow walking trail that went deeper than recognition, deeper than memory.

He stopped running. He stood at the edge of the

field and understood where his legs had brought him.

He was back in Cottage Grove.

His legs brought him back to the park. This was the park from the beginning of everything. The park he and Paige used to visit growing up. The park where he would take Emily.

It was also the park where he played soccer with friends; where he sprinted down the sideline as a teenager without knowing anyone was watching. The park where a man walked a young whippet on a leash and stopped because of what he saw.

He had not been back here since before he became homeless. He had not allowed himself to be back here. His body had not consulted this morning.

He stood at the edge of the field and something moved though him that he had no immediate name for. It wasn't grief or the bitterness he might have expected from standing in the place where everything had started. It was larger than any of those things and quieter.

His legs gave slightly and he sat on the grass at the edge of the path. He pressed both hands flat against the ground. The grass was cold and damp.

He breathed.

The memory stepped forward, quietly like it had been waiting for exactly this moment, in exactly this place, because no other moment or place would have been right.

The sound of a man who once stood on the edge of a field and saw that he was worth believing in.

"Relax your shoulders, kid. You're fighting the wrong thing."

His head dropped.

It was steady, practical.

"That's shaking?" coach Roberts said. "That's not fear. That's effort."

He closed his eyes and suddenly the world wasn't this park anymore. It was every park. Every track. Every sideline he had ever stood on with Coach watching quietly before speaking.

His chest tightened.

He breathed, waiting for the voice to fade. It didn't.

"You still have it," Coach said.

"I told you that the first day I saw you. Remember?"

In this field. Dolce tearing across the grass like freedom itself.

His throat burned.

Then the truth he'd been walking around for years crawled to the surface.

"I'm sorry," he whispered to the empty field.

Nothing answered immediately.

He didn't stop there because there was more and it had been waiting long enough.

"I should've come. I should've. I should've... I don't know. I should've shown up for you. You were there for everything and I..."

His voice broke on the word before he could finish the sentence.

"I disappeared,"

"You didn't disappear," Coach's voice said, with the same firm simplicity he had always used to correct form before correcting confidence. "You got hurt. That's different."

Jake let out a shaking breath.

"That's life, kid," Coach said. "Nobody teaches you how to lose the things you thought made you… you."

He nodded, his eyes wet, the grass cold under his hands, the empty field in front of him, the trail behind him that had carried him here without asking.

"I didn't show up when it mattered," he whispered. "Not at the end."

The silence came again.

Then:

"Okay," Coach said … the same way he always had in practice when Jake made a mistake. Never dramatic. Never disappointed. Just steady. "Then you start showing up now."

Then the thing that had probably always been true and had been waiting for the right moment in the right place to be said.

"You don't owe me an ending. Don't throw the rest away."

Jake sat. The park came back. The sound of wind through upper branches, the soccer field where a boy once run without knowing what his running meant. The voice didn't vanish. It stepped aside back into the place it had always occupied inside him, which was something more permanent than memory.

He looked at the field one more time. He pushed himself to his feet. The path was still there. He turned back, the way he had come. He didn't sprint. He jogged, carefully and without agenda, back along the trail he had run and every mile that remained.

Some mornings, the wind leans against him like a

hand trying to push him backward. Some afternoons the rain needles his face, turning the path slick and uncertain. Cold wrapped his muscles tight at the start.

He keeps showing up anyway. He's not rebuilding strength, has that. The fear still lives in him. Sometimes mid-stride, a flash of stadium lights slices through his thoughts, and for a heartbeat he's there again, hearing the crowd turn into a sound he never wants to hear again. His chest locks. His shoulders tense. His legs hesitate.

Nothing's wrong. Memory is the injury. He stops. Breathes. Grounds himself. Starts again. There are days he runs longer than planned. There are days he stops earlier than he wishes he had. There are days the only victory is lacing his shoes. Once, halfway along the path, he sits on a bench, laughing breathlessly into the wind.

"Maybe this is stupid."

No one expects anything from him. No one is watching. There's no scholarship, no contract, no future hinging on this. He could stop but he doesn't.

Then one afternoon, when the sky hangs low and the air smells like rain-that-hasn't-happened-yet, a pack of college runners comes through the park. They move in easy formation, shoes whispering over the path, laughing between breaths, strong, confident, young.

Jake is moving when their route merges with his.

They're beside him, he eases past them, just running.

One of the boys glances over expecting to see another trained athlete, not a weathered face, unshaven, layered in worn clothes. His eyebrows lift. Another mutters under his breath:

"Who the hell is that guy?"

No one chases him. They know he's fast. It wasn't in the past fast but still fast. Jake hears them but he doesn't look back. He keeps going. He can still do this because the engine isn't gone.

One morning soon after, he runs farther than he's meant to. No plan. No internal negotiation. He doesn't stop when the border appears in his mind. He moves through it like mist.

When he finally slows, hands on his hips, lungs burning, wind scraping sweat cold against his skin, he realizes what he's done.

He looks back at the path behind him.

Then it hits him.

A laugh. He bends forward, breath shaking, laughing.

Marc Cianfarani

Chapter Thirty-Nine

Emily lay on her bed with the room dark except for the rectangle of her laptop screen.

The search bar again.

The same name.

Jake Clark running.

She typed it so many times the browser completed it before she finished the second word. Old articles loaded, grainy race photos, old headlines she didn't remember reading, stories from a state she barely remembered. She hadn't been to Oregon since they left. Sometimes she wasn't sure which memories were hers or borrowed from the pictures kept in a shoebox on the top shelf of her closet. The shoebox she had never shown to anyone. Not even Mitch, who had been nothing but kind to her, who had shown up consistently and never once asked her to call him anything other than his name.

She clicked one image anyway; Jake crossing the finish line, eyes bright, smiling.

She didn't know him.

She only knew what Mom told her, which was careful, fair and somehow still incomplete. Like a story told around a room that nobody wanted to enter. She had stopped asking direct questions around twelve because she could see what it cost her mother to answer. It wasn't worth it. So, she learned to find things herself.

She opened the hidden folder she never mentioned.

One photo at three years old, sitting on his shoulders, both of them laughing. She zoomed in on her face first. Then his.

The Jaw.

The eyes.

Her eyes.

She had her mother's mouth and her mother's stubbornness and her mother's way of going quiet at times. But the eyes were his. She had known this for years. Looking at the photo now she felt it differently.

She closed the folder. Outside her window the city made its ordinary nighttime sounds.

Mom said they were going "To watch," in the voice she used when it was more complicated than the sentence it arrived in.

Emily had nodded said "okay'" in the voice she used when she understood more that she was going to acknowledge out loud. They were good at that, the two of them. Years of practice.

What Mom hadn't said, and what Emily had been sitting with all week, was the possibility that he might be there.

She had done the math herself. The race was in the city. Mitch was headlining it. Mitch had history with her father. Her mother had agreed to go without much resistance for someone who generally had opinions about how she spent her Saturdays.

She was fairly certain she was right.

She pulled up the registration page and scrolled through the listed entrants like she had every evening since Monday. Hundreds of names, she had read them all twice. She had not found his.

It didn't mean anything. She told herself that. People

registered late. People registered under variations of their names. People showed up on race mornings and paid at the tent and ran without being in any database at all.

The photo was still open in the background tab. She switched back to it without meaning to.

He was twenty-one in the picture. Younger than she could fully imagine him. She tried to picture him now, mid-thirties. She tried to picture what that looked like and couldn't quite get there. The face in the photo was too specific and too young.

She wondered if he thought of her.

She wondered if that was a naive thing to wonder.

She closed the laptop, letting the room fall back into darkness.

She lay there, looking at the ceiling until she was ready to sleep.

She turned onto her side, pulled the duvet up around her shoulders, and she whispered into the quiet, a wish she didn't expect to work, but one she couldn't swallow anymore.

"Please be there."

Marc Cianfarani

Chapter Forty

The mudroom sat off the garage, lined with white oak lockers build to pull sweat and dust out of the air. Shoes filled the shelves in clean rows, neon foam untouched.

Mitch sat on the bench with a brush in one hand and a damp cloth in the other. He worked at the sole of a trail shoe, digging into the grooves, flicking loose a bit of dried dirt.

Oregon.

He pictured the air first. Damp. Pine-heavy.

Then the track.

Then Jake.

The gym came back without warning.

Rubber and sweat, Timed sets.

Jake dropped to the mat and started pushups. Clean, full range. No wasted movement.

Mitch watched him in the mirror. Smirked.

Then set down what he was holding, crossed the room, and lowered himself to the mat a few feet away.

They started at the same time.

One. Two.

The rhythm locked in without either of them trying.

Fifteen.

Twenty.

Jake didn't break form.

Mitch kept going. Sort of.

Somewhere past twenty, his elbows started cutting the distance. The movement changed shape, became something else entirely.

Jake glanced over

Stopped.

Stared.

Mitch met his eyes and then it hit him.

He started laughing. Loud. Uncontrolled. He pointed at Jake, folding in on himself, the sound bounced off the empty room.

Jake tried to hold it together. Didn't.

"You weren't moving," Jake said.

Mitch waved a hand, still laughing. "I adapted."

"Thirty-one," Mitch said from the floor.

"Thirty-one," Jake said.

Mitch's hand tightened around the shoe.

Another memory, quieter.

Parking lot. Night air cooling off the track.

Two beers. No crowd.

Mitch talking France, Monaco.

Jake listening. Then

"You ran good tonight."

"You too."

The memory dropped.

The room came back. The shoe in his hands. The scuff along the heel.

Then the thing he didn't say. He could still see the

corridor. Indoor nationals. The guy from the circuit.

Whatever happened to that guy on your team? Clark? Jake?

Someone said he's been living rough. Like actually on the streets. You didn't know?

Words he'd been carrying since.

The shoe rested in his hands, half-cleaned. He stared at it, seeing something else entirely.

The door slid open behind him with a soft hiss.

"There you are."

Paige stood in the doorway, the kitchen light behind her. She looked at the bench and the shoes.

"I've been looking for you," she said. "Are you planning on cleaning every pair you own?"

Mitch set the brush down beside him.

"Making sure I've got the right ones," he said. "It'll be wet."

She stepped in, phone in hand.

"We need to book the flight," she said. "There's an early one through San Francisco or a direct at noon. If we take the early one, we'd have to wake Emily up at five."

Mitch nodded, but he wasn't looking.

"Mitch?"

He didn't answer.

She lowered the phone slightly.

"Eight fifteen or noon?"

He stayed where he was, eyes fixed on nothing.

The race. The city.

"Mitch."

He blinked and looked up.

"Where are you?" she said.

He let out a breath and the shoe slipped from his hands onto the bench. He stood.

"Paige," he said.

"What is it?"

He looked at her.

"There's something I never told you about Jake."

Chapter Forty-One

He found out standing in front of a bulletin board taped to the wall of a community center. Flyers overlap in layers, yoga classes, lost dogs, language courses. Then he saw it:

Charity Race Registration Now Open.

He stepped closer without realizing he was moving. The poster showed an image of a finish line. Faces cheering and runners in motion. And near the bottom was the Entrance Fee.

Entry Fee: $60. Registration closes soon.

A volunteer in a neon vest smiled at him from the doorway. "You running?"

He replied. "Thinking about it."

"Great event," the volunteer said. "Big turnout this year."

He gestured casually. "Bring the fee when you sign up."

Jake nodded, thanked him, and walked away. He waited until he was around the corner before he stopped and let the weight sink in. Sixty wasn't a number. Sixty was days of stretching food. Colder nights because he wouldn't spend on a blanket.

He starts working for it. These aren't jobs you fill out forms for. The work that starts before sunrise.

He swept the front of a convenience store while the owner fumbled keys in the lock. The broom scraped grit. He got paid with a folded ten and a genuine thank you. He carried crates behind a deli, hands raw from cold plastic. Nobody asked where he slept. Nobody asked why he looked exhausted. A man pressed money into his palm like a handshake.

He helped a café stack chairs after closing. Someone left a half sandwich "by accident" on the table near him. He wrapped half for later.

He slept outside every night.

Same park.

He tucked what he earned deep into his bag, wrapped tight in a sock. He counted in the dark sometimes, to remind himself he was not imagining progress.

Coins turn into bills. Slowly, they start to matter.

A man promised to pay him and never returned.

Someone called him "buddy" in the voice people used for things, not people.

The knee swelled and he wondered if this was foolish.

Every time that voice rose, he saw the number:

Sixty.

The money lived in a sock.

He kept it at the bottom of his bag.

Counted it once every night before he slept.

Ten. Ten.

Five. Five. Five.

Sixty.

It had taken him weeks.

He counted it again before bed, tied the sock closed, and slid it deep into the bag.

Rain woke him up sometime in the night.

It wasn't heavy but steady enough to matter.

He dragged the bag closer under the tree and tucked himself around it and slept again in broken pieces.

Before dawn he reached for his sock.

The neck was open.

He stared at it, then turned it over,

The bills came out damp and stuck together. He separated them carefully in the dark.

Ten.

Ten,

Five.

Five.

Five.

Five.

He counted again.

Forty.

He searched the bag first. Then every pocket. Then the newspaper he used for insulation. Then the wet ground around the trees, hands moving through mud and leaves.

Nothing.

By the time the sky started to lighten, his fingers were numb and dirty and he was still twenty dollars short.

He sat back against the trunk with the damp bills in his hand.

He doesn't sleep again.

Morning came gray and wet.

Jake walks. No direction.

He passed the community center and stopped.

The flyer was still up in the window.

Registration closes today. Entry fee sixty dollars.

He looked at the sign. Then at the money in his hand.

He went in anyway.

A volunteer sat behind the folding table. Reading glasses pushed up on her head. Clipboard in front of her.

"Hi there," he said.

Jake laid the bills down and smoothed them flat with his palm.

"I'm twenty short," he said. "I know that. I had it last night. I," he stopped. Started again, "I had the whole amount."

The woman looked at the money. Then at him.

"I'm sorry," she said. "We can't register anyone without the full fee."

Jake nodded.

"I know."

She waited.

"I earned it," he said. "that's all."

"I believe you," she said.

That made it worse.

Jake picked up the money, folded it, and put it in his pocket.

Then he walked out.

He moved through the morning without paying much attention to where he was going. He stopped in front of a sporting goods store. Running shoes in the window. Bright lights. Clean laces. White soles.

He stood there. Longer than he meant to.

Then an arm hooked across his chest and pulled him hard sideways into the recessed entrance of a closed laundromat.

His first instinct was to shove back.

His second recognized Ray.

"Easy," Ray said.

Jake looked past him.

Two police officers stood outside the store. One of them speaking into a radio. The other glanced once in their direction, then away.

"You were out there a while," Ray said.

Jake looked back at him. "What."

Ray raised an eyebrow.

Jake let out a breath. "Okay."

The officers moved on.

Ray waited until they were half a block away.

"What happened."

Jake leaned back against the wall.

"The registration for the race."

Ray said nothing.

"I had it," Jake said. "Last night I had sixty. Rain got it. Sock came open. I went in with forty."

"How short."

"Twenty."

Ray looked at him for a second, then reached inside his jacket.

He took out a folded cloth pouch with a rubber band. Slipped the band off. Counted bills into his hand.

Jake shook his head immediately.

"Ray, no."

"Stop."

"That's your money."

Ray held it out.

"How much you think I handed you."

Jake looked down.

A ten. A five. A five.

Exactly enough.

"I'll pay you back," Jake said.

Ray shrugged. "Then pay it back."

Jake didn't take it.

Ray kept his hand out.

"You running or not?"

Jake took the money.

They move, the weren't sprinting, but cutting

through side streets and across a parking lot down an alley Ray seemed to know by instinct.

By the time they reached the community center, the volunteers were beginning to pack up.

"Wait," Jake said, pushing through the door.

She looked up. Recognized him.

"You might be our last entrant,"

She pointed to a kid sitting at a table inside.

"He can help you."

Jake looked at Ray who was turning toward the door.

"Ray."

Ray glanced back.

"Thank you."

Ray studied him a moment.

"Don't waste it," he said.

Then he walked out.

A kid barely out of high school sat behind the table. Hoodie. Backwards cap. A half-eaten granola bar beside a pile of safety pins. He didn't look up right away, slid the clipboard across.

"Name. Age. Division choice if you've got one."

Jake stared at the blank lines.

Name should have been easy.

It wasn't.

He wrote slowly. His hand shook halfway through the last letter.

Jake .

He stared at it a second longer, like if he handed it over it would become real in a way he couldn't take back.

He slid the form forward.

The kid glanced at it. Then actually looked at it.

His eyebrows lifted a little.

"You ever run before?" the kid said casually.

Jake hesitated.

"Yeah," he said quietly. "Long time ago."

"High school?"

Another pause.

Jake shook his head.

"No."

The kid waited, curious now.

Jake's voice dropped without meaning to.

"College."

The kid blinked… then leaned back a bit, thinking. He turned the paper toward himself like it might look different from another angle. Then he stood.

"Hang on a sec."

He disappeared behind the tent flap.

Jake stood there, heartbeat loud in his ears, part of him wanting to chase the paper down and ask for it back.

Before the kid returned, the volunteer beside him tapped the table.

"Entrance fee."

Jake nodded, reaching into his pocket.

He pulled out a handful of crumpled bills, soft, wrinkled, worn, edges nearly torn. He flattened each one carefully on the table with his palm, embarrassed at how long it took.

The volunteer didn't say anything. Didn't smirk. Didn't pity. Counted. Nodded and dropped the bills into the cash box like it was normal. He set a wristband beside the form.

Jake didn't put it on. His hand hovered there.

For a second then he slipped it on.

The kid came back.

"Are you the Jake Clark from Springfield?"

Jake nods.

The kid left and returned holding a bib with a small gold circle stamped beside the printed name.

He set it down.

"Director said any D1 seeds or legacy names show up, they go in the first wave.

The kid slid it forward.

"Elite division."

Jake didn't touch it.

"I haven't…" he started. "In a long time."

"Still counts," the kid shrugged. "Some people sign up dreaming about standing where you're standing right now."

Jake reached out and lifted the bib. It was lightweight. Harmless. Paper and ink. Jake stepped aside, staring at the number in his hand. The gold circle caught the light and flashed. He breathed. In and out.

His hand closed around the bib.

Marc Cianfarani

Chapter Forty-Two

The city quieted past midnight. Traffic thinned to the occasional sweep of headlights.

Jake lay on his patch of grass, hood up, backpack under his neck, the race wristband loose around his wrist. He turned it once with his thumb and left it alone.

He didn't sleep.

The memories come out of order.

Springfield first.

The warm synthetic smell of the track in the summer, At the line, fear and joy so tangled he'd never learned to separate them. Back then his life had felt like an arrow.

Coach's voice came next. Steady.

"You don't run because you're fearless, kid. You run because you're scared and you do it anyway."

He let it pass.

Then Paige. Laughing at a comment he made, light catching her face. Being beside someone who knew the worst of you. He let himself have that. Then set it down.

Emily last. Heavy in his arms the first time. The grip of her fingers around his thumb. Certain and absolute, like she'd decided who he was going to be.

He reached into his back pocket.

Over ten years of folding had taken the paper almost to transparency. The creases had gone white. The edges had softened to the texture of cloth. His fingers found it without looking, they always did.

He didn't unfold it fully. He knew what was there.

He found it in the early days, when he began living outside. One of those nights when the cold came through everything and he'd learned to layer newspapers inside his jacket, close to the skin, trapping what little warmth the body still made.

The photograph had been large, centered impossible to miss even in the poor light bleeding in from the path lamps. Mitch in the middle of the frame. A small flag. The headline clean and celebratory above him.

And in the background slightly out of focus, Paige. Emily on her hip.

He'd taken it apart over time. Mitch first. Then the headline. Most of Paige.

What remained was a strip of background. Emily on her mother's hip. Small. Blurred at the edges.

A photographer who hadn't known what he was capturing. Preserved in newsprint.

He held it now without looking at it directly. Every detail was memorized. He thought about the twenty-four-year-old, who had found this and broken for years after.

He thought about all the cold nights he could have put it down and hadn't. He folded it back along its worn crease. Returned it to his pocket.

He didn't know what she looked like now.

She would be sixteen. He had done that arithmetic so many times it had become something else. The years accumulating into a list he could not stop keeping.

He had told himself, in the early years that staying invisible was mercy. That if he could not be the man he was supposed to be, the least he could do was stay out of the way. Not complicate things. Not arrive and leave again, asking them to absorb another version of what he'd become.

He had believed that.

He was not sure he believed it anymore.

Hiding had a cost. He understood that now in a way he hadn't when he was still explaining it to himself as protection. The cost wasn't his. He'd been paying with their time. With Emily's questions that someone else had to answer, or no one had, about where fathers go when they stop coming home. With everything Paige had absorbed and managed and carried in rooms he was no longer in, in ways he would never fully know.

He had not been protecting them.

He had been protecting himself from having to be seen as what he'd become. He knew that it took too long for him to realize this.

He turned the wristband with his thumb. Felt the ridge of the numbers printed on it.

Tommorow he will stand on a starting line.

He will wear this number on his chest where people can read it. He will move through the city in the open, in daylight, among people who will see a runner. Not a man with a grocery cart. Not someone to step around. A runner. He cannot undo the years or recover what he left on a windowsill in an apartment whose lock had been changed by the time he went back for it. He knows that.

But he also knows what he is running toward.

Not Mitch. Not the time or the result or whatever story the cameras want to tell about a charity race and hometown return.

He is running toward the moment he stops being

invisible.

And if she is there somewhere in that crowd, if Paige brought her, if Emily is old enough, if any of that is possible in a world he has no right to predict, maybe she will see him.

That is what he has. He lets himself have it. Then sets it down carefully.

The fear came. His chest tightened. He wanted to get up but he didn't. He turned onto his side, pulled his jacket tighter and breathed.

In. Out.

The city settled around him.

Chapter Forty-Three

The barrel was burning. Jake wasn't there.

Smitty stood with his hands out, turning them slow over the heat, shaking his head already.

"The place is gonna be swarming with cops," he said. "You're out of your mind."

Ray didn't look at him. He was working a piece of wood into the fire.

"Hear me out."

"I heard enough," Smitty said. "They cleared the encampments last time and who'd they come looking for? You." He jabbed a finger at Ray's chest. "They think you masterminded the whole thing."

Ray shrugged. "That wasn't mastermind. That was common sense."

"That was you getting your name written down somewhere," Smitty said. "You show up there, they're not clapping for you."

Cecil sat on the bucket, harmonica low in his hands. He played a few notes, soft, wandering, then stopped.

"I don't know," he said. "We're gonna stick out. That crowd…"

Rhonda snorted.

"What, you think they've never seen people before?" she said. "Relax."

Smitty shook his head again, faster now.

"It's about being seen by the wrong people."

Ray finally looked up.

"It's a race," he said. "Not a crime scene."

"Depends who you ask," Smitty muttered.

Cecil turned the harmonica once in his hands.

"I ran a race once," he said.

No one reacted.

"With my kid," he added. "Little league thing. Around the bases."

Smitty glanced at him "And?"

Cecil shrugged. "Nothing. Just… ran."

No one spoke.

Rhonda leaned forward, elbows on her knees.

"I'm in," she said. "Jake's cute. I like watching him run."

Smitty gave her a look. "That your whole criteria now?"

"Works for me so far," she said.

"I could make posters," she added. "Big ones. Bright. Make it look official."

"Where you getting that stuff?" Cecil asked.

"No one is making posters," Smitty snapped.

Ray stepped closer to the fire.

"It's not about that," he said. He paused. "He's one of ours."

No one spoke.

Ray went on. "He didn't have to let us in. But he did."

Smitty looked away.

Cecil tapped the harmonica against his knee.

Ray's voice dropped.

"Feels like a chance to show up for someone."

Rhonda shrugged.

"Speak for yourself honey," she said. "I don't have

any babies out there I'm trying to make up for."

The fire shifted. A log dropped in on itself with a dull crack.

Smitty rubbed his hands together, slower.

"Still gonna be cops," he said.

"Probably," Ray said.

"Still gonna look at us first."

"Probably."

Cecil lifted the harmonica. Blew a short note. Let it hang. Fade.

Smitty stared into the barrel.

Then he exhaled through his nose, once.

"Fonzie," he said.

Marc Cianfarani

Chapter Forty-Four

Race morning sounds like this.

Soft chatter layered with nervous laughter. Velcro straps. Shoes being slapped against pavement. Volunteers calling out instructions. A speaker crackling with music that doesn't quite fit the seriousness in people's eyes.

Jake stands among them. He's back in it.

Sunlight stretches across the street, turning breath into thin ghosts of mist. Color everywhere: jerseys, charity shirts, kids on shoulders waving signs. A looping course, the announcer keeps reminding them. Start here. Finish here. Same place. Same faces waiting.

Jake doesn't need the reminder. He rolls his shoulders and shakes his hands. He hears footsteps all around him, elastic, confident, familiar. The sound of people who sleep indoors and train in shoes that haven't seen winters.

"Elite bibs to the front, please!"

The announcer's voice carries above the crowd. Movement begins. A ripple of gold-circled runners drifting forward.

Jake stays where he is.

Someone taps his arm.

"Hey man your bib. You're supposed to be up there."

Jake hesitates.

Then he nods.

Steps forward.

But only to the back of the elite group, like he's

borrowing space.

He feels eyes on him. Curious. Maybe Confused.

Is he someone? Was he someone?

The noise tightens.

Then…

The horn sounds, and everything burst open at once.

They launch.

Elite bodies burst forward fast, as if pavement is optional. Jake doesn't chase. He settles. Breath. Rhythm.

Crowds line the barriers, leaning in, cheering anyone and everyone. Hands clap. Names are shouted. Bells ring.

"Jake! …Jake, go!"

A rough pocket of voices near the rail. Out of rhythm with the rest of the crowd. One of them shouting too hard. Another laughing in the middle of it.

Jake hears it.

Doesn't turn.

The sound folds back into everything else.

He hears his own footfalls.

Then.

A voice.

Soft at first. Uncertain.

"…Jake?"

Fifty meters ahead, on the right side of the barrier, Paige leans forward, hand shading her eyes. She didn't expect to see him. Didn't plan for this.

Emily hears her say the name.

Her head snaps up.

She looks. Searches. Scans the moving pack desperately.

And she finds him.

She doesn't hesitate.

"Daddy!"

The word isn't a cry.

It's a collision.

Jake almost stops.

The race disappears. The noise drops out. It's her face older, straighter hair, longer limbs but still her.

He breathes in sharply, the moment hitting his chest harder than any finish line ever has.

Emily is still yelling.

"Daddy! Daddy!"

He doesn't wave and doesn't speak but he runs.

Because he can now.

Mitch hears her too.

He turns mid-stride.

Sees Paige.

Sees Emily pointing.

He follows the line of her arm.

Sees Jake.

Mitch doesn't smirk. Doesn't glare. It passes through his face, shock, understanding. History settling where it belongs.

Then he faces forward…

…and pushes.

Too fast. Too hard.

He's not running strategic. This isn't pacing.

Crowd roars as he breaks from the group, pulling a gap. The announcer climbs in pitch. "Looks like Mitch Hughes is opening up early, bold move"

Jake doesn't chase yet.

He runs his race.

Body steady.

Breath clean.

Mind quiet.

He leans into rhythm instead of memory.

Runners begin falling behind him. One. Then another. Then a cluster. No drama. Steady. His stride lengthens like his body finally remembered what it was built to do.

Halfway mark.

Mitch has two hundred meters.

Jake takes one meter back.

Then another.

Crowd volume swells. People are screaming. Phones up. Kids banging on barriers.

Final kilometer.

Jake is tenth.

Then seventh.

Then fourth.

Mitch's shoulders tighten.

Stride stiffens.

Breath gets ragged.

Jake keeps gaining.

Four hundred to go.

One hundred meters left between them.

Mitch sees the finish arch.

Sees Paige.

Sees Emily bouncing and yelling and crying and everything at once.

His face breaks, not fear.

Conflict and relief tangled together.

Three hundred meters.

Jake is flying.

People see it now.

"Who is that?"

"Oh my God."

"That's…wait…that's Jake!"

Two hundred meters.

Ten meters between them.

Emily's voice slices through everything.

"GO, DADDY! GO!"

Jake hears it.

Mitch hears it.

One hundred meters.

They're almost shoulder to shoulder.

Fifty meters.

Mitch digs with everything he has left.

Ten meters.

The crowd explodes.

They lean forward.

Finish.

Mitch finishes first, by feet and stumbles catching himself.

Jake crosses a heartbeat later and collapses to one knee, chest heaving, laughing, breath breaking.

Emily runs.

Mitch opens his arms automatically, bracing for her.

She runs right past him.

Straight to Jake.

He barely has time to get to his feet before she hits him, launching into him like she used to when she was small.

He catches her without thinking.

His arms wrap around her and the world falls away.

She cries into his neck.

He closes his eyes.

"I'm here," he whispers. "I'm here, kiddo. I'm here."

Paige presses a hand to her mouth.

Mitch stands a few steps away, breathing hard, chest rising and falling. He watches them.

Jake looks up.

Their eyes meet.

They don't speak. Mitch nods, and Jake nods back.

The crowd keeps cheering.

Epilogue

The backyard was strung with lights Mitch had spent most of the morning untangling. Someone from Paige's office had brought a cake with the UC seal on it in blue frosting, slightly lopsided, which Emily had declared perfect.

Duran Duran played from a speaker. Emily had been obsessed for weeks. She and Paige were still arguing about John Taylor.

Jake arrived through the side gate with a card he'd rewritten twice, a bottle of Champagne and Bullet on a lead. The whippet stepped into the yard ahead of him, nose up, reading the air.

He stood at the edge of the yard before anyone saw him. Mitch noticed him first and raised his chin in greeting. Jake nodded back.

Paige was beside him a moment later.

"You made it," she said. Her eyes dropped briefly to Bullet. "Both of you."

"Told her I would."

She smiled, and crouched to let Bullet sniff her hand. Then she stood and touched his arm. "She's been watching the gate for an hour."

He found Emily near the table, mid-sentence with two girls from her class. She stopped talking entirely when she saw him.

Then she saw Bullet.

She crossed the yard in about four steps and dropped straight to her knees on the grass. Emily laughed, both arms around her, face pressed into the dog's neck.

"Bullet."

Emily pulled back enough to look at the dog's face. Bullet looked back at her and licked her nose.

Emily laughed again, louder this time. It was the laugh that Jake had carried with him through every cold night and every bad year. The one he had kept folded in his chest like the strip of newsprint.

She looked up at him from the grass, still smiling.

"She's perfect," she said.

"I know," Jake said.

She stood and he opened his arms and she walked into them exactly as she had at the finish line, without hesitation.

"Hey, Em."

She pulled back and looked at him.

"You're really coming," she said.

"I'll be there before you are," he said. "Probably make you run repeat four hundreds."

She laughed. "I'm not running track."

"We'll see."

Bullet, pressed herself against Emily's leg.

Mitch appeared with two cups and held one toward Jake.

"How are things going?" Mitch asked.

"It's different, I don't know how coach did it for all those years," Jake said laughing.

"You were the only one I thought of, when they called."

"Thanks for putting in the word."

"You're a lot more like the coach than I could ever be." Mitch replied.

Mitch raised his glass. Jake raised his and they cheered. Something passed between them that neither of them named and both of them understood.

The lights came on as the sun finished dropping. Paige was laughing across the yard. Emily was dancing to "The Reflex" by *Duran Duran* with the two girls from her class. Bullet was running around the backyard, her tail swinging in circles.

Later when the party thinned and people began leaving, Emily found him. Bullet was curled at his feet, finally still.

"I'm nervous," she said.

"I know."

"About all of it. It isn't just the school part."

He looked at her. She meant being in the city and campus where he walked around with a clipboard and a whistle as Assistant Track Coach. She meant whatever this new version of them was going to look like.

"Me too," he said.

She sat beside him on the step. Bullet stirred and repositioned herself across both their feet.

"But you're going to be there," Emily said.

"Yes."

"And you're not going to disappear."

"No," he said. "I'm not going to disappear."

She leaned her head against his shoulder.